Praise for

BROKEN MEGAPHONES

"I don't know many poets and mystics, but Andrew William Smith is the genuine article. His poetry exudes passion, and his vulnerability on these pages is nothing short of stunning. There is a deep religious fervor in these pages, unafraid of the call to abandon idols and name the violence inherent in religion as a weapon. Poets are often feared because their deep vulnerability can expose our dangerous illusions. Mystics find themselves marginalized because they see through our artifices. But we need them and their honesty. *Broken Megaphones* is witness and testimony, fire and love. It is a gift. Take. Read. Receive."
-Rick Quinn, writer at *PopMatters* and *Ordinary Space*

"America is facing a mass exodus from churches everywhere as a result of the ongoing abuse, bigotry, homophobia, racism, sexism, idolizing nationalism, and plain hate that the mainstream American church has clung to for decades. Andrew explores these reasons and more as he walks, runs, and plummets us into his own deconstruction journey. Jesus has left the church, and if that bothers you, infuriates you, unsettles your soul, this collection is for you."
-Chelsea Meeks, advisor and instructor

"In *Broken Megaphones,* Andrew Smith is the reincarnation of Lawrence Ferlinghetti. Ferlinghetti, who died in 2021, lived to be 101, but he didn't live long enough. Fortunately, Smith picks up the story where Ferlinghetti left off, after Ferlinghetti's Christ climbed down from the cross, and Smith takes us to the places Christ is going today. A Christian in spite of himself, Smith has seen the glory, and his poems are a reminder that once we've seen it, we don't un-see it, even when we close our eyes. He is a prophet for our own times."
-Martha Highers, editor of *Under The Sun*

BROKEN MEGAPHONES

Christ-Haunted Poems About
Loving & Losing Religion

ANDREW WILLIAM SMITH
(ANDY SUNFROG)

Ordinary Books

BROKEN MEGAPHONES:
Christ-Haunted Poems About Loving & Losing Religion
by Andrew William Smith

For more information contact:
P.O. Box 1150
Cookeville, TN 38503
https://ordinary-books.blogspot.com

Interior and cover design by Carolyn Oakley,
Luminous Moon Design, Boulder CO
luminousmoon.com

Published by Ordinary Books, Cookeville, TN
ISBN: 978-0-9772258-4-2

First Edition: June 2023

ACKNOWLEDGEMENTS

Special gratitude goes to my incredible book designer, Carolyn Oakley at Luminous Moon Design. I could not have made it to printing without her and my editorial readers, enthusiastic endorsers, and beloved creative supporters: Rick Quinn, Chelsea Meeks, and Martha Highers.

As always, I dedicate my creative works to my spouse Jeannie and to my friend and teacher Jesus, who especially sparks and haunts these poems.

Likewise, I thank and blame my mother Barbara and late father Kenneth, for raising me up as a faithful collaborator in the many overlapping circles of the Christian left, as the fertile soil of Beloved Community, growing from the compost of late capitalist speciesist white supremacist heteropatriarchy. So this Jesus is also the Holy Fool, a subversive prankster who surrenders his own authority to make common cause with the misfits on the margins, so we might theologically mock the faux morality and illegitimate authority of the religious far right. Moreover, I must acknowledge the last several years of social and political turmoil that are the moral underside to inspire every frantic insomnia keyboard stroke to pack these pages.

Finally, I am part of an ever-widening circle of colleagues and comrades, of fellow poets and activists, of preachers and theologians, folks with whom we share community and mutual aid. Locally in Cookeville, in Tenasi, I have joined forces with numerous collectives and congregations who are "doing the work." Thank you. Your names are wrapped around every corner of my existence and experience, and you have been there for the spiritual and creative co-care that keeps us going, with a special nod to the emerging "scene" at the Sawmill Poetry Series here in Cookeville, especially our curator and my colleague Erin Hoover.

CONTENTS

ABOUT THE AUTHOR

ALSO BY ANDREW/SUNFROG

FOREWORD

by Rick Quinn

On the one hand, religion seeks the ungraspable, the horizon beyond the horizon. On the other hand, it takes form in concrete material practices, words, and images because they are the currency we mere humans trade. The intractable tension between the two can be overwhelming. All too often, we choose what we can hold on to at the sacrifice of that which exceeds our grasp. Humans collapse finite and infinite to make this work, and we make idols out of our ideas. Why do so many constrict and ground ourselves against uncertainty and, ultimately, transcendence?

This collection of poems by Andrew William Smith looks fully into the abyss and steadfastly refuses to succumb to the move of idolatry and constriction. Even more, he refuses to stay silent about the violence and harm wrought by abusive forms of religion. More dangerously, he dares to raise the question of whether the abuse is baked into the mix. No flinching here. There is a holy boldness within these pages that will not be received favorably by those addicted to coercive authority and its attendant harm. They will see it as dangerous. It is. And it is necessary.

For close to a decade now, I have had the distinct honor of knowing Andrew. He is a dear friend, sage guide, colleague, and mentor. We met in 2013 at a conference on Emergence Christianity and bonded over our shared love of a favorite band. Over the years, he has generously invited me into his "magical mystery tour" through conversations, concerts, collaborations, and pilgrimages. I continue to be awed and inspired by this poet, prophet, teacher, preacher, DJ, and radical lover of life. There is a fire that burns deep within Andrew's spirit, a fire that leaps off the pages of this collection. A concoction born of his deep empathy and love takes him to places where others would falter because such a path embraces sorrow and joy without discrimination.

I don't know many poets and mystics, but Andrew William Smith is the genuine article. His poetry exudes passion, and his vulnerability on these pages is nothing short of stunning. There is a deep religious fervor in these pages unafraid of the call to abandon idols and name the violence inherent in religion as a weapon. Poets are often feared because their deep vulnerability can expose our dangerous illusions. Mystics find themselves marginalized because they see through our artifices. But we need them and their honesty. As a book, *Broken Megaphones* is witness and testimony, fire and love. It is a gift. Take. Read. Receive.

FOREWORD

by Chelsea Meeks

Andrew Smith has been a teacher, mentor, colleague, and dear friend to me for nearly a decade. I've known him as all of these things, but I have also known him as a poet and a preacher. Andrew taught me the healing power of poetry. He pushed me to engage with my own work in ways that I never thought I could. I gained my adult confidence through poetry when I needed it most because Andrew was in the wings with exuberant encouragement. This collection of poetry is a testament to that healing power of poetry. Andrew seeks answers, rages at the world, the church, and god, and encourages love above all else in these deconstruction poems.

Andrew and I met when I was beginning my own deconstruction process at twenty. I was one foot out the church door looking over my shoulder at the pulpit, and now I can't step foot in a church and only want to talk about religion academically. But I remember that Andrew was the first Christian I ever met that didn't believe in hell—a belief we share. We worked together to bring ideas from many faiths to young students just starting out in the world, and I think I learned more than they did. He opened up religion softly when and where it was needed most.

Now, with this collection, Andrew opens up the sometimes brutal and always challenging deconstruction process that comes with leaving the church you thought was safe and good. America is facing a mass exodus from churches everywhere as a result of the ongoing abuse, bigotry, homophobia, racism, sexism, idolizing nationalism, and plain hate the mainstream American church has clung to for decades. Andrew explores these reasons and more as he walks, runs, and plummets us into his own deconstruction journey. Jesus has left the church, and if that bothers you, infuriates you, unsettles your soul, this collection is for you.

PREFACE

The poems in this collection are all recent dispatches from a religious deconstruction that turned into revival. These deeply theological poems are the howling prayers of an anarchist-pacifist antiracist queer-affirming Christian fighting against the creeping Christocratic nationalism of my region, the stolen Cherokee land of Tenasi. These rants and chants chart my journey through religious deconstruction into the defiant redemption of the Christ who haunts the Bible Belt with an underground solidarity and witness of grief, hope, and human liberation.

Written from 2020 through 2023, the poems are shared in mostly chronological order to chart the months leading up to my decision to resign my pulpit as the primary pastor of a small rural and Protestant mainline church in middle Tennessee.

A year after walking away from that job, I resigned my membership and renounced my elder vows in the denomination that had been my religious home for eleven years, the denomination in which my parents had belonged for decades and where I had been active in leadership at the local, regional, and national level.

To be clear, at that time, I thought I was completely done with any organized Christianity, but through the workings of the Spirit I have found revival at the margins, in the "unchurch," in disorganized Christianity, if you will. My calling was not wrong, it just needed tweaking, as I find myself organizing, preaching, and pastoring at the margins, at the intersections of a few denominations in what I like to call the "anti-authoritarian Christian left."

Like its predecessor of religious poetry, my 2013 volume *Beat Is Beatitude,* this collection is as informed by the rants and chants of hippy Beat counterculture as by religious commitments. That fusion of church and counterculture has been an obsession of mine for years and will inform an upcoming prose collection of essays about hippy Christians. It moved me greatly when a new friend immediately discerned the profound influence of the late Beat author Lawrence Ferlinghetti on my poetic practice.

Friends often ask me why I stay in Tennessee due to recent politics, and I know I am called here, not just for the natural beauty and community I have found, but also for our place in the music scene and in civil rights history. The image of the megaphone or bullhorn had already attached itself to this collection before it became a symbol for the Tennessee Three, our embattled legislators speaking out against gun violence and bringing their bullhorn to the floor of the Tennessee General Assembly.

Another friend observed that they see my journey through the lens of what Flannery O'Connor called the "christ-haunted." Although I am by no means an O'Connor scholar, the enigma of Southern literature always percolates in my pages. In this collection, I realized how profoundly the "christ-haunted" description was needed, for the backstory behind the bullhorn. For backstory, O'Connor wrote:

> "Whenever I'm asked why Southern writers particularly have a penchant for writing about freaks, I say it is because we are still able to recognize one. To be able to recognize a freak, you have to have some conception of the whole man, and in the South the general conception of man is still, in the main, theological. That is a large statement, and it is dangerous to make it, for almost anything you say about Southern belief can be denied in the next breath with equal propriety. But approaching the subject from the standpoint of the writer, I think it is safe to say that while the South is hardly Christ-centered, it is most certainly Christ-haunted. The Southerner, who isn't convinced of it, is very much afraid that he may have been formed in the image and likeness of God. Ghosts can be very fierce and instructive. They cast strange shadows, particularly in our literature. In any case, it is when the freak can be sensed as a figure for our essential displacement that he attains some depth in literature."

While I have not included every poem I have written in the last few years, many do show up here. With each passing tragedy or attack on various communities, a new depth of commitment emerges. Some days we are fearless, but even when we are afraid, we keep on going anyway.

These poems are for radical left activists who want to explore their religious sensibilities, for preachers and liturgists who want fuel for their activism or quotes for their sermons, and as sparks for the many converging movements that seek to sustain a uniquely Southern and north American liberation struggle for all people and for the planet. And if you are reading these in whatever your context, I am offering these poems as gifts and as charges for you.

ANDREW/SUNFROG, EASTERTIDE/PENTECOST 2023

STOLEN JESUS

Look at that no evidence
No real motive
No relative sanity
No end game
But plenty of blame
They have stolen Jesus again

Selling grave clothes as another souvenir
Looking for internet articles
To prove that the end times are here
If you thought Judas & the devil were bad
These new evangelicals say
Wait just hold my beer
They have stolen Jesus again

Bodies are just bodies
Made in the image of God
But bodies were made for cages
Gun-toting rages
Sex with underages
The email incrimination of
An entire nation
They burned up all the pages then
They stole Jesus again

We would like to say it is only
The emperors
The kings & presidents
Blame the Baptists & the Catholics
the conservatives most of all but
Do we really have that much gall
To ignore the tweet in my own eye

As we watch the faith tradition
Roll over & try to die
We stole Jesus too
Trying to prove that my theology
is better than yours
We no longer ask ourselves
what would the savior do

I cannot give this rant enough heft
for the right or for the left
For the people who want Mars &
their electric cars
Forgetting always the one
who hung the stars
It makes this sober drunk
Want to head back to the bars

Everyone is stealing Jesus again

This might be the best case
to give in to my base
urges & purges & just throw all
this recovery away
This might be the best reason
For heresy & treason
For anarchy & atheism
For Buddhism or just ordinary sin

But then I hear an inner voice
crying don't give up so easy
You can find me hiding behind the cross
Counting my blessings
Recounting my loss
Giving zero days notice
To every human boss

Disappointed in the church
The schools & the state
But trading my theology
for a pint of grace
& loving fate

Brewing some more coffee
Writing some more poems
Hitting a few more meetings
& opening up that weathered leather tome
To the verses that we memorized as kids
Forgetting for a moment what Jesus would do
& just studying what He did

THE MAN CAUGHT IN ADULTERY

Do you remember the Bible story
about the man caught in adultery?
Me neither

Not that there were not men in the Bible
I mean men committing adultery
in the Bible times

But there just is no story like that
Just the woman caught
& almost stoned to death

do you remember that story
in the gospel of John about
the woman caught in adultery

& the man named Jesus
who helped to set her free
by writing in the sand

They say King David did some bad things
That King Solomon had a lot of wives
But King Jesus

this is a different story
about a man who took the woman's side
who listened to the women

sadly not the nameless woman
raped & murdered
in the book of Judges

but the supreme Judge is now
giving mercy
to the woman

the woman
he is believing & listening to
the woman

looking at her as a person
listening to her as a victim
loving her as a human

that woman in that story
in the Gospel
according to John

but what about
that man
caught in adultery

in acquaintance rape
in clergy sexual misconduct
in "I thought it was consensual sex"

when it wasn't
what about him

why don't we have a Bible story where Jesus forgives him
maybe it is because the woman
about to be stoned is the one who really needed help

maybe it is because in patriarchal society
we don't stone men to death for
doing what men do

it was just a boy being a boy
it was just lockerroom talk
it was how the world works

it is not wrong if the woman at the Trump rally
wears a t-shirt that says
I want him to grab me by the

patriarchal self-loathing
context is everything
dominant culture too

So what about the man
caught in adultery
he has a job

he is the breadwinner
he has a scholarship
he was the captain of the team

what about his career
what about his reputation
no no no

what about his power
it is
it was

it will
always be
about his power

King David
King Solomon
King Trump

but not King Jesus
he is talking about the women
he is standing up for the women

you say you follow this Jesus
you say you worship this
Jesus

but you stopped saying
what would Jesus do
a few years ago

because it doesn't
support the
celebrity rape culture

the male entitlement culture
the white fragility culture
the scholars say the story about

Jesus supporting that woman
caught in adultery was added late
was an editorial correction

but if it was added late
they could take it out early
& write about the man caught in adultery

the sports celebrity
the TV celebrity
the megachurch celebrity

the man caught in adultery
said he was sorry
besides she asked for it

she wanted it
she doesn't need to be
in the new Bible

where we no longer listen to victims
where we require them give birth
to the babies of their rapists

don't listen to King Jesus
be like King Trump
rewrite the Bible to always forgive

the man caught in adultery

DIAGNOSIS

chasing the place yes the last place
where surrendering
from self-destruction ends
& self-care begins

chasing the last tailpipe
of temptation & turning from
chaotic crude credentials
to a difficult diagnosis

diagnosis gives vocabularies
to the visions
words to the wild wonder
category to the crazy

of what feels like a normal
of caffeine meditation
treadmill transformation
sauna saturation

how do regular people manage?
they still drink & we still dream
sober but surreal
surrendered but standing still

THE GEARS OF LENT

throw myself on the gears of Lent
just another broken sinner
barely hanging on

ashes to ashes
dust to dust
maybe not must

the professors debating
a more humane atonement
stuck in their laptops

but ours is a liturgy of
chaos & mud
corpses & sin

the dirty earth opens up
& takes another
another body in

sometimes we need a Jesus
of the earth & on the cross
not just one in heaven who sings

you struggle with every task
yet pretenses of piety or perfection
are your internal joke

because it is a miracle
to just get up every day
to refuse the booze & the coke

powerless after powerless
codependent too
throw me on the gears of Lent

where it is not only
about me but also about You
when You are part of us

WHEN THEY LYNCHED JESUS

Were you there
when they lynched Jesus
Were you there
did you carry the nails

Did you like the crack of the whip
did he get what he deserved
did you sip the sour wine with the soldiers
did you tweet this at 1am

the only good Nazarene is a dead Nazarene
& when the prophecy starts
the crucifying starts
Christ ain't nothing but a thug

were you there when they lynched Jesus
did you watch the temple burn to the ground
did you praise Roman law
did imperial lives matter

did you care a thing for the Jews
were you there when they lynched Jesus
if you were what did you say
they are still lynching Jesus

his name is George Floyd
her name is Breonna Taylor
his name is Ahmaud Arbery
his name is Martin Luther King

the truth it may bug you
but our Lord is a thug too
were you there when they lynched Jesus
& now what are we going to do

COMMITTEES IN THE HEAD

I am neuro-diverse
anxiety & addiction & ADHD
sometimes all the committees

in my head show up at the same time
with a loud agenda
hate consensus

& have no idea what
parliamentary process is
& don't always know

the difference between
self-harm & self-care
so don't Google all that

shit like spiritual bypass
like imposter syndrome
like the finest pinpoint

of an interfaith
within an interfaith
a theology within

a theology within
a philosophy within
a political identity

just looking to let
off some steam
at some intersection

out past my sanity
where some book
or some idea

or some song
will make it all
make sense

when the loving
your enemies thing
is not working

when the revolution
thing is not only
on Twitter but

this is a pandemic
did I wash my hands
& wear a mask

Covid positive after
the protest sent
the fear right down to

my toes just because
asymptomatic what else
nobody knows

HATE THE HIGHWAY

hitchhiker
heretic
hell-raiser

but trying so hard to be bad
didn't work so now
I try to be good

but in the upside down
world of a fascist white
power fantasy

what the fuck
is good anyways
righteous rant

that
this
is

radical hobo punk
send me back to
the poetry bootcamp

can't tell the difference
between the on-ramp &
the off-ramp

hate the highway
anyways except
when it gets me

the hell
out of
here

GOING DOWN

not a hurricane
or the holy spirit
heaven help us

not even a plague
or a riot or
a murder

not a hundred protests
in a hundred days
in a hundred cities

not the veterans &
the active duty saying
he is full of shit

nothing seems to phase
the king surrounded by
blonde robots reciting

a loyalty oath
to a fake flag against
real anti-racism we are all

hunkered down
on Twitter
killing trolls

with a glorified typewriter
but there is not glory
in this gory murder

of children in the street
hey hey
what's that sound

vigilantes & cops
order flags unfurled
what is going down

EQUALITY GOOD NIGHT

just wagging your weapons
like that makes you a man
but aren't you the the type
to throw someone like me
in the back of an unmarked van

posting fake Facebook stories
like QAnon crap is the same
as Jesus in all His glory
ignoring actual history
with your wounded pissed
poor white man mystery

shouting rights rights rights
while you take off your mask
then steal a woman's choice
after you rape her
you never ask her consent
even as you overcharge rent

Just to live in these bodies
then wonder why we vent
they burned up the idea
of any big tent

then Breonna & George &
John Lewis & RBG died
is it any wonder why
we are all feeling fried

but now is not the now
to say equality good night
now is the time to dig in
& fight fight fight

HALLELUJAH FROM BELOW

drip drop dreary drift
to some other fascistic horizon
we scream "no"
we sing wake me up when September ends
we count the days until November begins
in this life too short
but this term too long

should we settle for another
serving of warm shit
just because we've been
taught it is better than
we deserve

I don't know about you
but we are lazy gluttony
we are gorgeous loony bins
so sure if you insist on
talking about original sin
even this consumer concrete
cavernous cell with cable TV
is more than we we deserve

but looking at lethal lecherous
popes & pimps & presidents
could we be both so humble & so bold
to chant together like the
most sacred of prayers

fuck this shit

we deserve better
we want better
we demand better
we are better
get it got it good

we want endless banquets
we want exploding bouquets
we want erupting bounty
we want eternal booty
we want everything because
we want equal becoming

so shut your
what about
this or that
your tit for tat
we are more equal
than all that

this is not the social media
shamefest olympics for
hashtag pushups &
rhetorical gymnastics

lack of power is our dilemma
tired of crumbs
tired of just another
piece of the pie

yes you can cry
yes we might die
but we are not interested in any of
your damn sugar sweet pie or
any other narcotic trick to
dope us back into submission

this is the mission
we are taking over the bakery
we are firing the boss
we do not have to justify your profit loss
we are redistributing the pain that you have
administered to the poor without account

we want a year of Sunday mornings
a jubilee to follow quarantine
a pollution-free hike to the summit of dreams
some universal basic inspiration to every person
regardless of belief in your broken promises
regardless of the churches with their
plastic capitalistic gods

we are done
with the demons & the devils
of your permanent deceit
we have seen the ledger even
as you burned the receipt

give us the access code
the password is still hope
we are done hacking the interface
we don't know our place
we didn't write the rules
that you impose but never follow
got to let your fields lie fallow
we harvest the blood of our martyrs
& take down every one of your terrorist flags

tomorrow is today
now is now
wow is how
universal buzzwords
regain their meaning
when your buzzsaw
economy crumbles &
we finally sing
hallelujah from below

A GOOD YEAR TO VACATE RELIGION

imposter syndrome
down the sudden robes
cannot hide the sin

the shame we could not
name comes
back to scold anyways

you saw an article
in a Christian magazine
that suggested you picked

a good year to vacate religion
it was about
a famous evangelical

on the massage table
with explicit details
of multiple accusations

so much sexual confusion
is the induced delusion
of our electoral intrusion

in the sexually repressed nation
of a presidential masturbation
& a woman-hating woman

to preside at another
judicial negotiation why
does she get the nomination

in the land of scandal
every word an abomination
yet nobody will believe

the civil disobedient
protest or negotiation
always the loser

in our analytical
prostration where
we forget

the platitudes that
they have the guns
but we have the numbers

why do you have the guns too
on your Facebook
Instagram

just because you have the guns
doesn't mean you have
to plan the first shot

they interviewed the militia
then they interviewed the
protester & guess what

you don't have the means
for "by any means necessary"
they kill we lose

we need a different plan
by gosh I have no idea
what that is nobody

signed up to be an innocent bystander
collateral damage
human shield

friendly fire in the
first civil war of this year
next year we might not

be here
because they said we were going
to steal the election

then they stole
the damn
election

they said we would
start a civil war
when this very

executive itself
has been a civil war
since January 2017

worst case
alarmist or nothing
else before the

last cry
last call
when every voice is muted

prayed
spoken
begged

on this last day
to register to vote
for the November election

WITHOUT ANYTHING

undiagnosed neurodivergent
from an anarchist jurisdiction
unrepentant from things that are not sins
don't judge my depiction

sing singing out the rings
from the bell
at the gates of the heaven
that looks most like hell

they have soured the taste
slip in our own waste
just another head case
running out of toothpaste

before the revolution
stuck in this nightmare
unraveling without anything
like a hopeful solution

DON'T LOOK AWAY

don't look away
no not yet
rearview mirror
horror before
the cosmic reset

they are taking
red pills for
communion wafers
worse than the abyss
a pure evil MAGA kiss

white hats &
army slogans
websites that look like they were
made for Netscape
back in 1997

I guess we are all
just so desperate
to belong we chant
where we go one
can't say the rest of it

addicted to new vocabulary
like deep state
false flag
psyops
do some research

which means watch so
much YouTube that when

you can't sleep
your brain explodes faster
than your soul erodes

so this is where we are
crackers with platitudes
trying to repair that
which is so broke
we can never fix it

but everyone knows
the fraud is the fraud
the false flag is the false flag
sorry not sorry but
losing is still a drag

so maybe today is not victory
but soul saving relief
for half the country &
the rest of the
whole damn world

CONVICT US ALL

Jesus come on
can you convict us all
me & my fellow followers

with a conviction so deep
devastating & real
convict us to feel

children in cages
grown folks in cages
drug dealers in cages

violent leaders
nonviolent offenders
Jesus convict us that

we were wrong
were wrong about being wrong
flip flop underground upside-down

Jesus convict the MAGA preachers
the mega church false teachers
convict accusers & accused

twist the twisted
uncurl the hair
unlock the snare

HATE SPEECH AGAINST HATE

so calling a racist a racist is racism?
so calling hate speech hate speech is hate?
hold my coffee this is way too late
haters gonna hate so much until they

break us with their lies
their Facebook echo chamber
of fake danger jelly rolls
their trolls gonna troll
it's just how they roll

down is up
up is down
enough hate to go around
every college town

they don't want
the big government in their lives
but they will sic the boss
yes the cops

sic the human resources
department on you
they seem demoralized maybe you
can be demoralized too

they don't want
the big government in their lives

unless you are a woman
unless you are black
unless you are queer
for you the police leave you
forever in fear

the civil war of 2021
is coming to get you
we don't care what you do
we only care who you are

leftist
commie
liberal
antifa
socialist
hippy radical witch &
every outspoken woman
is just a
bad word
to them

talk a good game of liberty
they got their small dicks
& their big guns & amen
the insurrection of January 6
was just good Christian fun

for patriots with liberty envy
& penal atonement theory
where Trump lost the election
to save you from my sins
of taking a knee

saying Black Lives Matter
saying Trans Lives Matter
saying anything but the
alt-right alt-lite
all white party line

Back in the 90s
with Al Gore & TennCare
I couldn't wait to
move to Tennessee
with "Tennessee Jed"
playing in my head

Now I have been a season & it's
you I accuse of unholy treason
I thought you bled orange
I thought you loved the Vols

until Black athletes marched
until Black athletes took a knee
because they want every Black person
to finally be free

to walk down the street
to never fear the heat
the vigilante or the cop on the beat
raise my fist never accept defeat

they used to say they loved the Big Orange
until the Big Orange wore black
now they just hang another noose
or shoot us in the back

like their lynching
great granddaddies
& their klan
such a reprehensible plan

is this how you prove
that you are a man
by threatening the youth
by just hating the blacks
by hating the queers
by taking
your orders
from outdated fears

The signal is buffering
you can't see the suffering
the page won't load
but what do you know

by wrapping yourself up
in the confederate flag
now you won't listen
to our siblings in drag?

just a small college town trying to party
like it's 1963
like it's 1953
like it's 1853

So you bring your guns to defend some statues
So you bring your guns to threaten elected officials
& their spouses & children
So you threaten teachers

So you run the liberal preacher out of town
Try to baptize with hate
but we are swimming
we refuse to drown

"Our blacks like it here"
you said it like a real cracker
& to be clear "I watched
this one Candace Owens video"

so now I am expert on Interracial Relations &
did you see my selfie with Herman Cain &
please don't let this poem die in vain
until we forget the Appalachian pain

of coal miners & sharecroppers who
could always fight together against the elite
a day might come when a cause much better
than your Trumpist lie will unite us in the street

Do you remember
Never forget
Slavery Lynching Segregation
Mass Incarceration

I was watching Bootsie Plunkett talk to
Jamaal Bowman on
Stephen Colbert
on February 25th

Congressman Bowman said
we used to be called "white allies"
but now we are accomplices
so Bowman asked for

co-conspirators & I said yes
Arm to arm
linked together
will fight racism until my death

Solidarity with my lineage to
Viola Liuzzo
James Reeb
Ken Smith

From Chicago to Selma
From Atlanta to Detroit
We got all that
We got your back

But also from Memphis to Knoxville to Nashville
From Chattanooga to Cookeville & back
to Lookout Mountain or Fall Creek Falls
fascism & racism are bound to fall

listen to the
young people
don't hide
behind the steeple

because when I was in high school
I believed that band
from another land
when they sang

do you remember this jam?

"People are people, so why should it be
You & I should get along so awfully?
So we're different colors & we're different creeds
& different people have different needs

It's obvious you hate me
though I've done nothing wrong
I've never even met you
so what could I have done?

I can't understand
What makes a man
Hate another man
Help me understand"

we will understand
raise our hands
until we forever abolish racism
in every corner of this land

VERSES AFTER GIBRAN

wonder when the regret is
greater than the wrong
regret the justice of the law
regret the heart of the guilty

we are but one person
standing in twilight
between our former self
& our better self

one stone in the church
is not higher than the
lowest stone in
the foundation

what the animal
that loves its yoke yet
sees the elk or deer as
simply stray or vagrant things

who hates dancers
who hates bodies
who hates weddings
who hates feasts

we feast for freedom
feast without laws
we are the sunlight
we are moon

out past the shadows
the growing edge
the expanding earth
turn to face the sun

travel with the wind
unlock the prison door
dance without chains
block nobody's path

they can muffle the drum
rip the strings from the guitar
but they will never
stop us from singing

GET BEHIND ME STATUES

Get behind me statues
stunning silence on the sin of symbolism

Get behind me stupid
shocking lack of looking deeper or learning to listen

Get behind me fake religion
comfortable cracker jack jacked up lack of Jesus

Get behind me bigotry
belligerent bruises against black & brown bodies

Get behind me intimidation
fear & lies & loose cannons of yours & mine

BROKEN MEGAPHONES

suddenly the self
is required to
check all his

strident hallelujahs of
sad raised fists &
broken megaphones

stuck in front of
Logitech computer
camera broadcasting

from home
praying from the
quarantine zone

the fight has
fought my anxiety
& fueled it at

the same freaking
time so when the
questions are asked

my morality tasked
some sentiments basked
in the revolutionary

baptism by the
waters of Babylon
linked arms to

liked tweets from
empty parks to
crowded Knoxville streets

now that I have
started again I
cannot stop this

water flow this
sacred hope of
praying with our feet

SOLIDARITY MIGHT BE EASIER

solidarity might be easier

when everything sucks this much
when every dumpster is on fire
when every boot is on every face
when every gun is jabbed in every back

when we stop arguing for just a moment
about the .01% on which we disagree
when we all are ready to join the athletes
who are ready to take the knee

when sometimes the knowledge from the
books you've read & they haven't isn't the hill to die on
when we realize that we are still the siblings
with so much in common that they always want to spy on

when we will lean on every lyric
every song & every movie to cry on
locking arms & raising fits
& getting ready to fight on

SACRED GRIEF

the sacred grief of
Rumi after Shams disappeared
Joni after Woodstock ended
The Dead after Jerry died
Altamont after Meredith Hunter
the revolutionary choir is here for
the hymns of hope & heartbreak
as we pulse & spin
until the walls crumble
& everybody is in

LIMITS

do i have limits
to my empathy
are we now required
to feel sympathy

for fascists
to walk a mile in
the abuser's shoes
i have no idea why

I still pay my dues

LOVE YOUR ENEMIES

Jesus we need to talk about all this
"love your enemies" bullshit okay
was it a little bit different back in your day
this is not a theological game I want to play

we are living with fascists & racists
sexists & homophobes who love to
claim you are theirs like
you are their biggest bro

now like my sponsor said
I am praying about this all day long
trying not to let the devil
live rent free in my head but

hard to tell the difference anymore
between being awake &
being in bed more difficult to find the love
for the fascist motherfuckers

who want us all dead

WEIRD RELIGION

all the people
who like to
pretend that our

religion ain't weird
super kinky strange
but what about that

torture device around
your neck &
what about your

sunday filling bellies
with symbolic
zombie cannibalism

don't get me wrong
because I am here for
all the weird

but pretending this
faith is boring functional or
normie normative is such

a silly joke
we are all mystic crazies
psychedelic hippy strangers

YOU DO YOU

Wake up wrestling with myself
deny your guts
ignore the voice inside
stomp on your instincts &
at the same time
just tell the truth
to thine own self be true

he said I was running
imagine younger me
breaking five minutes for the mile
he said I was running but
the way I saw it I was sinking
slowly in quicksand choking
on insects wrestling with rodents
dying slowly on the inside
to thine own self be true

in trouble for being outspoken
then asked not to speak
what did he say
interrogation not conversation
I am the subject of a
company's internal investigation
to thine own self be true

just be cool
you got this
we'll be fine
well fuck that
I am fire
I ain't got nothing

fire like the California wildfires
ice like the ice caps melting
lost like the oceans rising
none of this is fine
none of this is mine
to thine own self be true

so from that posture of
desperate emptiness I
wake up
to the morning
wake up
to the cloud dawn
to thine own self be true

under-published poet sucking
dreams from the sky
complicated married monk
motor city slave to the funk
defiant activist sober drunk
believer in the free lunch
to thine own self be true

not calm
not carrying on
but connected to the ground
to the land that is not ours
we are all reckless refugees
planting flags on moons we
never really knew
to thine own self be true

so everything I mean everything
is temporary
just a glance of chaotic chance
on the wind that blew through
yes a bunch of angelic seed-pods
stardust swirling hairless monkeys
evolutionary consciousness junkies
animated Adamic atomic dirt
breathe life into me
to thine own self be true

you do you
what does that even mean
you do you
I don't know who
made up that phrase
but it must be a phase
stop being so spiritually
intellectually ideologically
theologically lazy
this is we not me
to thine own selves be true

me doing me is
not only fighting fire with rhetorical fire
it's also everywhere everyday ecstasy
dancing barefoot in
circles to the Grateful Dead
or many other bands too
you do you boo hoo
but I don't know who
to whom
I am being true

Jesus or Buddha or
Mom & Dad or
the writings of Diane diPrima
Thomas Merton
Walt Whitman
or the tree on my walk that we
hungrily hug every single time
I walk right by it

just tell the truth
when the truth is
an explosion that would
render this illusion to dust
to tell the truth we must
stop joking
pretending
half-assedly hoping
I am not naked
before a firing squad

& still laughing
even as the climate is
gasping grasping
grappling with solo self
but don't forget the
cosmic self that
these tired soul-sucking
suits left on the shelf

wake up
whisper desperate prayers
of the powerless
but just remember
the powerful are
powerless too
but at least we wild-eyed
hopepunk dreamers &
crazy mystics
at least we know powerless
know it from licking
the rock bottom
of existential reality
where we get our lessons
from chunks of gravel
shards of glass
or blades of grass
we get our lessons
from the stones
from the saints
from the stars

THE FREIRE DARE

"Education either functions as an instrument which is used to facilitate integration of the younger generation into the logic of the present system & bring about conformity or it becomes the practice of freedom, the means by which men & women deal critically & creatively with reality & discover how to participate in the transformation of their world."
—Paulo Freire

I have a dare that
you remember Freire
that first time you
studied *Pedagogy of the Oppressed*
back in grad school

do you dare
remember Freire

dare that you
go there
to live remembering
how unfair
it was to be laughed at
or judged for
accepting food stamps
while teaching college

dare that you
go there
to remember
qualifying for
every tax credit
but never paying

taxes for causes
you hated simply
because you were
another professor
below the poverty line

Dare to Freire
remember to care
that the debt
that the fees
that the new construction
& all the needs
of the academic beast
can trace their
lineage to those things

colonial
imperial
carceral
industrial
settler
racist
militarist
capitalist

even though you are sober
from booze how long
have you been drunk
on your own humanitarian
impulse that your
white male tenured privilege
is a victimless crime

remember freire
take a dare
to know that most
of your colleagues
really don't lose sleep
thinking about this shit
take a deep inhale
to abandon any attachment
to your status as a

tenured radical like
armchair leftist professors
before you

remember freire
if you take this dare
grow back your hair
learn not to care
what the haters say
on any given day

when always already
to empower the students
was never about any coercion
or carceral model of
graded exclusion
some arbitrary ranking
the greatest delusion

who were the propertarian people
who convinced us that we spend
even one second of our too short lives
with a plagiarism checker
with speculation about an 18-year-old's
motive when submitting an essay
for my required undergrad class
when they are here surviving
a pandemic education & are perhaps
seeking more meaning & human mentoring
than worrying about punishment from
a poorly paid poorly equipped member
of the pedagogy plagiarism police

let me just throw plagiarism on the fire
or on the compost heap throw it out
with the pretensions of academic freedom
& the idea that we need face-to-face conferences
in corporate hotels
flying on corporate airlines
polluting this dying planet to present
a paper about ecology or theology
to ten people sipping bad coffee

out of disposable cups or chugging
bottled water from a plastic chalice
that is killing the ocean

let us throw all that away
& all the used copies of the MLA manual
or the Harbrace Handbook let me just
toss them all on the bonfires of our
endless arrogance & hypocrisy

remember Freire do you dare
or will you ever care that the
subjects you teach by necessity
always include their own obsolescence
in the red hot passion of
real poetry &
real revolutions
so get off your tenured high horse
sure this may be a form of so-called livelihood
but teaching was never your life

if you remember your Freire &
your bell hooks & your Vaneigem
& CrimethInc too
it was never about
a career it was
never about you

& now that you remember all this shit
stop your crying whining fit
for we have a world on fire
species committing mass suicide
not to mention homicide & ecocide
on an unimaginable scale
so if from this job you bail
there is more work for the people
than saving your ego or pride

& now remember in your bones
that over the four decades of your
engagement in this movement
you have only taken different drugs

from booze to theology to a well-paying job
to self-medicate your healthy outrage
at the horrible moral cost
of being an American
of being a white person
& if some racist internet trolls or
local fascists talking shit on Facebook
in speculation about your
morals or motivations is the
consequence of cutting ties
with peace for the sake of peace
when there is no peace
so be it

but that university you ever tried to love
this university or that university has
never ever had as a real function
but to
uphold the society of
slaveholders
prison builders
war makers
body haters
money makers
land takers
& religious fakers

do you dare
remember Freire
then you won't care
what happens with this complaint
or the job which was never more
than a temporary coat of paint
like some aesthetic makeover
& cheap deodorant
to cover the rusty dirty ugly smelly
multicolored reality of life bursting
from within itself at the
wondrous imaginal seams

that you got away with whatever
minimal good within that system

for as long as you did: brilliant
just another scam like when
you had to crawl in a dumpster to eat
or drive-&-dash without paying
just to get to the next town when
you had to steal the books you
wanted to read instead of pay for them

please don't kid yourself
wages are not remuneration but
the language of
transaction & inaction
exploitation & domination

don't be such a cheap date Sunfrog
whatever time you got left on this
earth is so freaking priceless &
the world of our dreams is still waiting
& like Saul Williams said on
that *Adbusters* mixtape back in 2002
we pledge to make it real

EXCOMMUNICATED

exile
exvangelical
extra in the wild

back from the journey
still a mess still
a work in progress

betrayed once
bitten twice
older brother syndrome

what ever gloss
you give that
drop kick & toss

it is all the same
shit if you still
need a boss

so we will
be fine
in the land

of wild geese
closer to fine & consumer
of non-alcoholic wine

see making treehuggers
subordinate to dead trees
is doing it wrong

the man they murdered is
more interested in the social
context of the murder

than He is in
damning
the trees

so older brothers please
hit stop say freeze
smile say cheese

stand on the mountain
feel your heart
on the breeze

players on their knees
schools with
their fees

a surplus of creeds
deficit of deeds
people still bleed

crybaby cry
feel your feelings
even the lord had to die

EASTER IN HELL

so it is the black
predawn between
saturday night

& sunday morning
yes
exactly

40 days ago
I got a memo
that turned my world

upside down
implied a threat
to end something

that I thought
was good &
provided me food

still vague I know
but that
does not change

that I could
lose two jobs
in less than a year

this does
not
change

that three minutes
before the service yesterday
I got a text from a "friend"

calling me out as
a protest pagan like three times
like the anonymous

message from the
day before
saying hey

"god
hates you
faggot"

& in the months
before I am a
"charlatan Iago"

or a "psychotic"
"deranged"
"goon"

not just
"off my meds"
but a

"fascist"
"terrorist"
"woke bully"

so yes if I
identify with
Jesus in Hell

with Lil Nas X
yes that is what
I said

it ain't no
thing about
a stripper's pole

or a hole
in the ground
like that tomb

where they
placed the
carpenter lord

the wine-maker
bread-baker
power-breaker

brown rabbi savior
preacher healer
tramp & Jew

who knew
that they meant all
that stuff about

the cross
who knew they
were not kidding

so this morning
I will rejoice in
all this persecution

as my friends keep saying:
like the prophets before me
damn Jesus this is hard

but yes even in
the dark of early
Sunday morning

the moon sets
& the sun shines
somewhere

to the
east
because it is

already Easter
& you better
flipping believe it

I am ready
for some
resurrection

CHRIST CLIMBED DOWN AGAIN

[after Lawrence Ferlinghetti,
for Lawrence Ferlinghetti 1919-2021]

Christ climbed down
from that lynching tree
& this season he never
ate in the upper room
because that was on Zoom

Christ climbed down
to walk away from
atonement theories that nobody understands

Christ climbed down
to tell the preacher to stop hating on sex
all the time

Christ climbed down
to tell the poet to stop making free verse
that rhymes

Christ climbed down
from that electric chair
& never cut his hair

Christ climbed down again
like Lawrence Ferlinghetti said
to remind us to banish all the liars
from inside your head

Christ climbed down
from every Christmas tree

Christ climbed down
from every Easter testimony

Christ climbed down
to march with Black Lives Matter

Christ climbed down
to dance with Lil Nas X

Christ climbed down
to steal a car from Joel Olsteen

Christ climbed down
to rebuke Mike Huckabee

Christ climbed down
to talk about the pagan themes of Easter
on your podcast

Christ climbed down
to watch that Easter video
released by Maynard from Tool

Christ climbed down
to earth
to hell
to your hospital bed
to your cash registers at big box stores
to the Amazon picket line in Alabama
to the biker bar
to the 12-step meeting
to the crying children who are sick of remote learning
to the protest against the Line 3 Pipeline

Christ climbed down
to cancel any idea of heaven that
excludes your enemies or
exists somewhere other than here

Christ climbed down
is totally loud
annoying
possibly female
never on time
refuses to pay taxes
or get a drivers license
or take weekends off
darn neurodivergent
workaholic lord
breaking his Dad's
own commandments

Christ climbed down
to love everybody
feed everybody
heal everybody
to be so honest as
to piss off Christians &
everyone else too

EXHAUSTED

exhausted
examined

unpacked
untangled

this energy has been waxing
yet been entirely taxing

protect me for tomorrow
as I receive my second vaxing

if there is nothing more to my prayer
I so appreciate your backing

with friends like you & Jesus
spiritual needs not lacking

pray through the day until dusk then dark
pray as I awake too early past midnight hark

sometimes I will get discouraged
sometimes I will be afraid

but something has come to my rescue
something strong is here now to return

to my roots to my hope to my source
to my soul drinking deep from inner force

take a breath keep fighting
this thing will run its course

COMFORT CURSE
—dedicated to my parents

all this comfort is a curse
do you remember that day
you were supposed to go to the zoo
but somebody snatched your mother's purse

this comfort is a curse
success was a drug that bought us
an indoor swimming pool but one day
my parents decided they would not be

mere moneyed upper-middle-class fools
I was almost 23, they were almost 50
Dad took a sabbatical in 1989
Mom joined him
in intentional Christian community in Chicago

they walked away from that creature comfort class
they were taking on a counterculture lifestyle
walking away from country club status
meeting Jesus among the poor
but also among those committed to
justice peace revelation
consensus conversation
radical disciple transformation

they were inspired in part by my time
at the Open Door Community just
two years before
just walking the streets
not only serving the poor
but choosing to be poor

inspired also by when
Daddy went to Mexico
with other church leaders
to Cuernavaca & learned about
the base communities there
from the Cuernavaca Center
for Intercultural Dialogue on Development

where poverty &
liberation theology were
in the ground & air

somehow the company of Dad's downtown
success decided it was best to buy him out
just like that
retired so young
but Mom & Dad
they are way better at math & saving
than their ADHD-poet-son
would ever be
so just like that they were free

suddenly such a shock to our systems
this changing landscape of our lives
they came home
they wanted me to meet a lesbian preacher
her name was Jane she would be my teacher

free from the tyranny of career & success
no longer participating in this particular principality
but continually confessing exactly what it was
they had savings were able to travel to
play cards swim in coral reefs take a
dinghy to an island off the island of Ireland
same island years later where Luke Skywalker would live
in the never-ending Stars Wars world

so sorry that Dad never lived to see those later films
he would have loved bragging that he was there
before Luke he would remind me that he took Arthur
& me to *A New Hope* when it first came out back
when that episode four was episode one

now that was fun so incredibly young we don't
know what we know now

about the curse of comfort
but they were learning all along
from Chicago riots to Cleveland witness
they were anti-racist church goers all the way back
raised us in integrated schools with fewer white than black
church was in a house & they called it the
Congregation of Reconciliation
1972 in Parma
Ohio some Presbyterians trying
to respond to the sea change of civil rights
racial reconciliation is still only an aspiration
at this hour in this situation so strange
like the boots of hate stomping on every flower
of joy & revolution & the family of hope
choosing instead cable news *YouTube* lies
a different more devious dope

they just walked away in the early 1990s
how was that like
more than 30 years ago
they were like
we will just
go with the flow
trusted their God to know
so into the throes of church reform
they were reborn with
religious feminists & queers
lobbied for universal health care
single payer like Bernie Sanders yes
but they were international in concern
traveled to Palestine
each radical step to disinvest themselves
from so many illusions of success

the credentialed actuarial career proper
only lasted Dad just 20 years
after years of training
but the retirement revolution was
24 years of grace

leaning into his calling in Detroit
that was always our place
where we were taught
to love God's black & brown face

Not his Parkinsons
not my alcoholism
nothing could stop us from following that Jesus

you studied at Chicago Theological Seminary
that Jesus you learned about when you
shared the room with Karl Barth
William Stringfellow
Martin Marty
Howard Moody

not to mention the wild Steve & Lois Rose
that Jesus you kneeled with in Selma
that Jesus when you marched for Caesar Chavez
that Jesus of the rainbow scarf
we wore at General Assembly
that Jesus of Palestine & peace marches
that Jesus of church camps where even evangelical
Jesus was radical to us
that Jesus every Sunday & like they say down here
whenever the doors of the church were open
that Jesus found in *Sojourners*
Dorothy Day
Ed Loring & Murphy Davis
Bill Wylie-Kellermann
The Other Side
that Jesus you unwittingly taught me through
music & television & art just by exposing me
encouraging me
going to U2 concerts with me

you taught me with those albums
Bob Dylan
Odetta
Joan Baez
Pete Seeger
& of course the speeches of Martin Luther King Jr.

I would just sit on the floor &
listen to him preach & I would cry
I would cry but also memorize
I would play the speeches over & over again
felt utterly robbed that we were only together on this earth
for six months now I can only imagine how his
widow & children were feeling then & now
& his only granddaughter so many years later

over these long years his cadence would become my own
thanks to so many friends & their hospitality
the black church became my church too
in this wild spirit ride
Jeremiah Wright
James Cone
James Lawson
Jesse Jackson
Al Sharpton
Otis Moss Jr. & Otis Moss The Third
I could go on & on
do I need to go on & on

that comfort was a curse
nobody cares that someone stole my mother's purse
or even today that I was beaten near death just
for being outside a car on those urban streets that I still love
that I cannot fathom as the gentrified reality that suddenly
descended where we used to get drunk
explore the ruins & listen to punk

where last summer the media missed the crazy
police state repression of Black Lives Matter
& with the city's police chief &
William Barr & Donald Trump surveying
the streets of my city from a helicopter &
discussing what only God knows but
I cannot imagine it was Black Liberation
this is why we fight march sing
dance protest preach
teach reach please

to remind people the difference
between the Selma kneeling which is
the same as the Kaepernick kneeling which
is the same as the ETSU kneeling &
we will never forget the Chauvin kneeling &
that some of you "sick white siblings" to
paraphrase Martin
actually chose
cops over Floyd
Pilate over Christ
you sold your own soul
bet on the Lord's clothes
& still roll the dice
with even the salvation of this
disgusting depraved
excuse for a nation
hanging in the hearse
will we end up in hell or
keep fighting for resurrection

yes that comfort was a curse
but this struggle is blessing
that is how Jesus is still messing with us
he preached & prayed & even praised
while crucified
because no nails
no nasty emails from people who learned
about me yesterday on Fox News
no travails can compare
with the reckless dare of taking
up our cross with you
with you my Mom & Dad
with Jesus my only Lord

yes comfort is a curse &
don't wait for the hearse &
nobody cares about that day
they stole my Mom's purse

COUNT IT BUT JOY

count it but joy
every barb & every blemish
who knows if this is the day
when you will say it is finished

but even tomorrow or ten
or twenty or thirty years more
we will keep going
endure the high calling

shake off self doubt
loathing lack or fear
but instead
count it but joy

DEBT

privilege is a debt
that is what the article said
staring back at me
for every eye to see

chains of moral debt
hanging from the nation
privilege is not a plea whose
maintenance will make us free

nobody wants to hear it
because it abandons the high ground
but here my thoughts are bound
I am a racist too

neither guilt nor shame
nor lies nor pride
explain all these police murders
describe how these siblings died

no I am not racist against whites
like the trolls will tell me
during burning July nights
defending whiteness ain't my fight

no this guilt is not built
I walk not on stilts
just crawling on my belly
shedding all that skin

shame blame
came the name
construct dialogue
outside the frame

the lie in the garden
was never sex or desire
come on people
there is another fire

the evil one's lie in Genesis is
their lie in the gospels it
is always the same old lie
which is why we die & die

lack of power is our dilemma
power this power that
power just another prize
at the bottom of the hat

oh I thought I was
such a cool cat
sickness is the selfishness at the core
self-care without ego such a bore

but the disease of me or thee
will never make you free from
the powers or principalities or
show the forest or the trees

so superstitious
so spiritual
they said your weakness is strength
empowered on your knees

so like a religious fool
who was never cool you
surrender again to fight evil
without a weapon in sight

walk into the warzone
unarmed with only
gospel songs or poems
filling your heart to overflow

to lose one battle
only to face another not
caring if you win but
love overflowing the brim

LACK OF POWER IS OUR DILEMMA

was this supposed to be perfect
I don't think there is a chance of that
when they come running for my body
a hangover or a blankety-blank baseball bat

seems the sorry state we are living in
the veil is always showing thin
call that for the powerless when they
talk about power not sure what they mean

go back to that early diagnosis of power
authoritarian & political & military
that is not power even though
they think it is can you dig

but somehow spiritual power or woo
woo happy clappy woo there is
power within that gets you up in
the morning & shows you what to do

then there is that power we get
when we sit in a circle & hold hands
& forego plans & smash aluminum cans
to say I am an alcoholic addict somehow sober man

then the power seeps up from the ground
into my feet my muddy toes watered
by the goddess I stand in the dirt
just watching my hair grow

such a messy silly crazy dancing
twirling spinning hopping frog of
neurodivergent hope & joy some people
don't need drugs because we are

this smashed effed-up wasted twisted tore up
crazy all the time all on our own so join a rebel
misfit secret society of 12-step drunks who pretend to
be monks show me how to live without forgoing my funk

5/2/2021 — 12 years abstinent today

NO SAFE SPACE

descendents of the colonial mind
need to stay uncomfortable there
is no safe space for stolen place

what if your wild retribution fantasy
were applied to your family in rape
massacre carpet-bombing boom

how grateful are you that you never
got what you deserved but that does not
mean you bully with toxic turbo grace

because white Jesus ain't no cosmic Christ
is the same as cold colonizing crackers
told you once told you twice what you

don't like to hear because it confirms
every one of your fears about what-the-
what are appropriate paybacks for

inherited sins that we so-called Jesus
people are suddenly so allergic to even
discussing the facts that your Lord was

brown or red or your God is black so if
white evangelical megachurch power trip
has its grip around spineless neck your

gutless body your soulless corpse
of walking lies you drink the potion as our
homeless addicted POC savior still dies

BROKEN PENTECOST

here is some potion
did they offer you some
unspoken agreements
I actually made none

the only contract
is in your head
if you want to lie in it
then make this bed

actually no I did
try to sell my soul
but they handed it back
just another broken bowl

just another refugee
just another fugitive
just another discarded
something something

bad words they sing
bad words they bring
now i am here for the sentencing
i am here for this thing

oh the illusion that
we could sit at the
big kid table i did
go to drink

at that mansion just once
but I felt like the
one in the corner with
the hat that said dunce

far too few people in the
polished room sucking
all the air I thought this
must surely be my doom

I never signed up for this
oh of course you did
every middle class white
boy at some point signs

their balls into a box
just punching the clock
click click end user
click click tick tock

but once I was inside the game
the hall of mirrors
the rush of blood
the feelings of shame

I forgot my baptism
I forgot my foreparents
I forgot my calling
I forgot my name

so no more shame or blame
I am just resetting the game
breaking the clocks
showing up like a flame

to burn this illusion once
& for all to the bloody
pentecost ground finally losing
myself so myself gets found

NO COPS IN THE KINDOM

ain't no cops in the kindom
your Bible never says
back the blue
you racist fools

I am calling out white people in general
I am calling out racist ass cracker fascists
in the most general sense because when
I name names they attack my very name

with death threats & endless blame
I got you I got your
stupid racist game so not talking to
any racist in particular but to all y'all racists

how stupid you were to attach
those flags to a cross
your idolatry is
everyone's loss

Jesus is a crooked crook
guilty of every anti-authoritarian
crime of which he is accused
if he isn't a guilty outlaw

then he ain't the anti-Roman
revolutionary rebel Lord he is just
an empty husk of nothing
with no salt no angelic light

definitely not white
you are so stupid to wash
his holy brown skin in
every racist sin

you built an entire religious
system based on guilt about
your genitals & passions
but such is your stupid racist fashion

that we can never feel guilty
about killing all the indigenous
forbidden for feeling guilty for
stealing the Africans from their land

bringing them here in chains to make
a bunch of stupid sinful rich crackers
who then paved over paradise for a
bunch of ugly cars & burger joints

they say I am racist against myself no
fuck your cracker jack redneck ass
just calling foul on your 500 years
just calling due the bills on your

endless trails of tears I am
pouring out all your beers
taking your stupid white cracker ass
to rehab to stop killing black people

stop preaching revenge
stop preaching God's wrath
there is not enough blood in your
cowardly bodies to pay the debts

on your racist imperialist sins
you better beg Jesus on your knees
because it is only grace that will save
your racist hypocritical face

CRITICAL RACE THEORY

such a day of restless remembrance
I cannot see it like some other day
could not get into the Bob Dylan day yesterday
because I thought with trembling about today

I cannot convince myself to call or email
senators Hagerty & Blackburn the blasphemers
but I am grateful for the people with
an inner constitution to call or email them

not like any of this will do any good
not that explaining Critical Race Theory
will help those who are bashing Critical Race Theory
not that explaining the difference between

white supremacy or anti-blackness with
the garden variety "reverse racism" being peddled
on the right will convince anyone on the right
to drop the pretentious pomp & admit they're wrong

should probably just stay off social media today
should probably remember there is no pentecost fire
burning outside my window & this is more like
Ash Wednesday on a Tuesday in late May

while we still wait
for a nation
to confess its
collective sins

ANATOMY OF A POLITICAL SPEECH IN TENNESSEE IN THE YEAR 2021 OR 2022 OR 2023
[with annotations]

Jesus Jesus Jesus Jesus Jesus Jesus Jesus Jesus Jesus Jesus is
my personal Lord & Savior
[It is important to say the name of the Lord as often as
possible with little to no reference whatsoever to what He
actually did or said]

My family family family family family family family family
family family my wife & kids
[heterosexual a must, white a bonus]

Something about the sanctity of life meaning the unborn
Something about the second amendment in close unironic
proximity to talking about the unborn
[see *Handmaid's Tale*]

The flag flag flag flag flag flag flag flag flag flag the military
the cops the wars & don't forget the flag

Then lay it on thick with lots of buzzwords like socialism
radical liberal leftist probably something mean about
transgender people & don't forget the taxes & the budget
[it is always the taxes & the budget when the other team is
in charge yeah we can always talk about balancing the budget
but never cut the spending on the military because the flag]

SEQUEL TO THE PRODIGAL SON

the sequel to the prodigal son
turned out strange because you
see the generous fabulous father died
& the older son took over the family land

the prodigal is still the prodigal
is falling down following unfollowing
from feral hovels to hearty feasts
no longer falling at Dad's feet

prodigal son got renewed for
another season things are not
looking good for him when
the older brother has been

talking to some people
some people are saying
some people are texting
some people are sending emails

some people are filing complaints
some people are calling the cops
because the younger brother
looks different acts different

younger brother had a relapse
younger brother is sleeping in a tent
but older brother is paying the taxes
older brother is covering his assets

nobody wants to hear a story about
how the prodigal left home again
or is happier making his own choices
rather than his brother who are we to judge

when we throw the younger brother
a dollar at the offramp
we are stressed but can't read how
blessed or messed up anyone else is

sometimes coming home is
only to leave home again
then the turning of the wheel
of life is free from older brothers

finally liberate us
when again we are free
to be free
again

PERSONAL GOD

so that personal "god" or is it "God"
has not been working out for you

because some have turned It into a genie a gadget
a magic 8-ball charm bracelet spiritual commodity

the personal god is too much like personal profit
personal preferences personal transactional salvation

maybe the impersonal god does not give a crap about
your "God things" but offers crap like golden gifts

raining on the believer as on the unbeliever
doesn't matter if you are an atheist because a theist

is just an atheist with a space
between the "a" & the first "t"

that idea of a higher power so central
to everything is lining up as nothing

or is it religion that has you kicked
to the curb sweeping soul sewage no

seeking God with your metal colander at
the bottom of a waterfall not catching a drop

feeling exiled from that first century rabbi
who was maybe just a mythopoetic template

of a pagan mystery god anyways but feeling
lost from that guy not because of that guy

who is love & rebellion & music
no that guy is fine

but because of guys in general because of
all the neo-reformed theobros on Twitter

because of church polity or church authority
or church hypocrisy or church survival instinct

so you remember this man wrote a book about
fire theology the whole place is on fire

I don't want to read that book again but the
earth is on fire & the only way to save us

is to leave the planet? or to engineer the atmosphere?
not a bucket of water big enough to drown all our

collective anxiety massive sorrow unprocessed
grief due to so much godly arrogance or greed

so you remember this one theologian okay damn
you are still talking about the theologians but

he talked about "the ground of all being"
like the interconnected rhizosphere beneath us

like you saw that lattice of light in a vision
like a net of light & dark or of sky & dirt

like nothing you know & everything you have ever known
like each tree you hug & every hike you have ever taken

like all the creatures even frogs & lizards & snakes & like
the green movie creature said life its energy surrounds us

"Luminous beings are we, not this crude matter."
"You must unlearn what you have learned."

Thich Nhat Hanh taught us about "interbeing" & just
like that we are interrelated interconnected interspiritual so

I have spit & spent
so many words chasing people & principles

to be downed & drowned
by impersonal principalities

forgetting to see that even within all that hot mess we
are part of it never quite escaping the endless glorious

beautiful stupid terrible tragedy of it because with it is
fantastic hopeful connection in spite of disconnection

unlearning learning with
that spacious empty long & winding

endless path with that bicycle
basket of a journey inside & out

FROM HERE

sometimes
I don't know you
but that
you know me
on this we bet
we hang our hopes
on this
we wager
everything

the distance
of mystery
so long it
defies measurement
a width so wide
we can't talk
about it
like we talk about
the exact time of sunset
or high tide

first time in
a strange forest
its familiarity
floors me
astonishes humbles me
a fierce
weeping earthling

so all this
lunar solar
martian talk
of galactic
significance fine
but I am here
for the mud
for the rocks
even the bugs
the summer of soft landing
in the sand of
our inheritance

you are not from here?
are you sure?
we are all our ancestors
is the earth not heaven
with feet or rocks
or cells or
however you want
to say it:
incarnation

sacred mama
celestial
terrestrial home
the biosphere
the biodome
ecology
earth house
gaia true
the only place is
the only planet for me
what about you

I want to be compost
when I die
my body that is not
is this to deny
our resurrection
but rather to say
maybe we do

join the stars
maybe the spirit soars
maybe the spirit soup
really is a different
dimension altogether

which means
this time
this crime
is refusing to
accept or
acknowledge our
profound earthiness
our creature nature
this undeniable yet
unbelievable
bounded gravity
tree & rock &
animal-like humility

humble
like the dirt
from dust
we come
& to dust
we shall
return

WE HAVE ALL THE RECEIPTS

We have all the receipts
for your religion gone wrong

purity culture for female parishioners
rape culture for male pastors
suicide hotlines for our queer siblings

We have all the receipts
for your religion gone wrong

justifying slavery
genocide or war just so you
can kiss the ring of Rome

We have all the receipts
for your religion gone wrong

some of us may still want
to repent or testify
to come home

but you have rendered the
church of our parents
into a hatefest for

hypermasculine
heterosexuality
on crack

We have all the receipts
for your religion gone wrong

I was a preacher until
I said
Black Lives Matter

I was anointed until
I told Caesar's thugs
to get off my porch

Now I am just another shameful
leftist without a pulpit or a robe
They act like I should have known better

than to actually expect these crackers
to believe in real truth spoken to real power
or to ever have my pinko hippy back

the American church is married to American power
you feed the beast the blood-soaked clothes
suckle the nipple of mammon every hour

We have all the receipts
for your religion gone wrong

now to get things really clear you are
demanding that we do not wear a mask
is there no limit to your bootlicking task

children are dying from Covid all around you
but you would rather we all get sick than
admit that your freedom fest was no such thing

they don't really want us to learn
they don't even want us to sing
it's just one poke in the arm

that didn't really sting

DECONSTRUCTED AGAIN

I didn't mean to get
deconstructed again
I was already deconstructed back when

back in the late 80s & early 1990s that's when
a postmodern primitive
was dancing with Pan

I didn't mean to get
deconstructed again
after I rode deconstruction into debauchery &
drunkenness until I blacked-out blind even at

Dylan
Springsteen
& the Jacket

After all those years I was fine
to be reconstructed resurrected or redeemed
however you want to call it
I was here for Jesus on a t-shirt
here for the cake the cookies
the punch at the reception

I didn't mean to get
deconstructed again
I didn't give at the office
or on Sunday morning
once again I've paid my tithe to rock-n-roll

Deconstructed without a high horse or
high ground or anything to hide me
but at least we have a kayak
life-raft on these rumbling rapids

No denying it anymore
just put my money where my fandom is
not just supporting the artists but
as one of the artists just said
we support the roadies & the crew
the people who plug stuff in

I didn't mean to get
deconstructed again
but the demolition crew was coming anyway
our world soaked in willful self-destruction
so much defiance of decency
denial of fossil fuel addiction
& dumbass maskless decadence

I didn't mean to get
deconstructed again
no wonder I sought a moment of peace
an inner monastic for a time this elastic
but we will not suffer an ocean
filled with boiling plastic
we will break

I didn't mean to get
deconstructed again
I would have been fine with a regimen of holiness
& look I'm just a big hypocrite
a revolving door of lost & found &
apparently lost again but at least
yesterday's theological pursuits
introduced me to universalism

I didn't mean to get
deconstructed again
but it's heaven all the way there
even in the middle of hell
an escalator going up up up

but not like Bezos in the sky
not like booze getting banned on flights
but please just let me get some sleep
we cannot afford to be up all night

I didn't mean to get
deconstructed again
like every back alley backstage rock bottom
once I puked in someone's costume hat
but when I listen to my sober dudes
like Jeff like Jason like Trey
will definitely make it just
one more day

I didn't mean to get
deconstructed again
or to get in touch with that radical past
more clear-eyed though this time
But I don't always make it to yoga class
My reading list is too varied & too long
my practice of my values too inconsistent

I didn't mean to get
deconstructed again &
while I may be leaving religion
I am still prone to preach
the pesky blood of the lamb
with another lesson to teach
about solidarity with those that are suffering
about no quarter for the super rich

I didn't mean to get
deconstructed again
in case we haven't noticed
there's still plenty of pain to go around
& I got deconstructed when
I got in trouble got that surveillance picture
on the front page to cast my lot again
not just with the marginalized but in the
sanctuary of the criminalized on the
other side of the bricks

I didn't mean to get
deconstructed again
born again was the same
I just want to dial things back
to however many first times
like when an old man
killed a rattlesnake in your road
& the fear of seeing another
rattlesnake the next day
left you feeling anything but old

I didn't mean to get
deconstructed again
like when the amplifier stacks were breathing
purple peace signs raining from the sky
Jimi Hendrix & Jefferson Airplane suddenly made sense
every question was answered with another question why
& even though life was shamelessly living itself
it was like the veils were lifted to the other side

I didn't mean to get
deconstructed again
back to when the feelings were free
crawl back to start with
scabs on these deconstructed knees
delete some more files
unplug other devices
reboot without apology
desperate for another analogy

I didn't mean to get
deconstructed again

PRAYER OF CONFESSION

I confess that I will miss the confessions

I confess that I am an imperfect
hypocrite bundle of contradictions
so keep that in mind during this confession

I confess that I am going to miss
the collective prayers of confession

I confess that I am going to miss
the gobs of guilt & collective accountability

I confess that no matter how effed up & wrong
& basically immoral the church can be
at least the religion of my foreparents
comes prepackaged with this
rubric of repentance & righteous truth-telling in
the face of wrongs
even their own

I confess I want my congressman
my state representative
my outwardly religious governor
who has banned CRT & demands opt-outs
for school mask mandates to read
this William Stringfellow quote

"For Christians, if for no others,
corporate social guilt is a
central biblical theme. It cannot,
therefore, be rationalized
or put aside."

I confess that all this is exactly what these entitled enraged
shameless suburban white anti-mask anti-CRT
anti-woke anti-social-justice
hey-just-get-over-slavery & genocide "liberty" fiends
what they keep getting wrong

is that your "personal morality"
or "personal responsibility" bit is
precisely about you admitting
it is your fault & finding
your part your role in it

I confess I thought it was so wrong when a few
years ago that these types would say stuff like
LGBTQetc Christians were fake Christians or the
same for lefty liberal pinko progressive or
whatever believers in the lynched Lord
like who are they to say who is or is not a Christian
but these days some of them are just so loud

I confess I get it when we say this current crop
of hoodless KKK moms & raging experts on herd immunity
are exactly the heretics
that white American evangelicals have always been
& while there are threads to their predecessors
there is something new about

this crappy crowd where those former adherents to
original sin don't really do sin they don't do guilt
it's just not their fault nothing is ever their fault
they are perpetual innocence for no reason whatsoever
& now they want to murder other white children
rather than admit that they are just plain wrong

I confess I don't see anything conservative about them
not much personal responsibility
in the personal responsibility crowd

I confess I am going to miss the cross going to miss
preachers quoting Paul with a straight face saying
that it is Christ & him crucified

I confess I am still clinging to the cross going to leave
them up around my house going to remember what I
learned from
Godspell & Jesus Christ Superstar
& MLK & Malcolm X

But when I watch that video of Metaxas whining about
being asked to wear a mask at a ski resort as proof that
the so-called liberals are the real fascists can I just
confess that I am done done done with your entitled white
Jesus forever & a thousand days

because Christ has Covid
Christ is female
Christ is queer
Christ is black
but most of all
Christ is intubated ventilated sick & in the ICU

see Jesus is everything
most of these Christians hate & have always hated

I confess that I am grateful that so many of my friends
have listened to that podcast about Mark Driscoll &
maybe some reckoning about the demise of
macho rape culture in at least some segments
of white Christendom but I will not be gracing the doors
of your megachurches & church plants to find out
how much confession & accountability you actually preach

I confess though that I didn't hear once in that podcast
that quote by Driscoll about not worshiping the
hippy queer pacifist Jesus because Mark Driscoll
refuses to worship a guy that he can beat up

I confess that this makes it all come back to me
about the macho middle school guys & their
macho middle school dads & their vast firearm
collections & that even in the 80s they were like
yes you can watch movies like Rambo with lots
of violence but you cannot watch any movies with sex

Because this is the core sin needing confession
from the white American church forever:
violence guns rape & homophobia

Jesus is always the guy that you beat up
Jesus is always the bullied never the bully
Jesus is the kid getting made fun of today
for wearing a mask in a school filled with
maskless teachers & maskless peers

Jesus is the guy & the girl & the nonbinary fluid person
you always hate or beat up or murder

Jesus is also Japan in 1941
Jesus is Vietnam in 1971
Jesus is Nicaragua in 1981
Jesus is Iraq in 1991
Jesus is Afghanistan in 2001 & 2021
Jesus is what imperialism isn't

I confess that I still dabble in church
hop on a little zoom here
listen to a radical podcast there
sarcastic lefties on Christian Twitter & Facebook
you are my jam

I confess that I am still very interested
in the Eucharist
Communion
Lord's supper
what have you
because it is mysterious & embodied
but especially among the people
that admit its similarities to
cannibals & vampires yes

But I confess I am
also listening to Buddhists
atheists SBNRs & nones
also dancing always
a spinner a whirling dervish
what is an alienated theologian to do

I confess that I will miss
the confessions & even the guilt
but never the shame
not all guilt is toxic or counter-productive
sometimes it is a cold shower wake-up call
because the whole universe is
begging us to pull our heads from
our posteriors & embrace some change

I will miss the confessions that say
we confess we don't know everything
that more will be revealed
that even the Bible says there are
infinitely more unwritten books in the spirit
that your religion knows nothing about

I TOOK COMMUNION TODAY

I took communion today
during a YouTube service
or was it Zoom

or was it Facebook live
I might have watched church
while running to Kroger

I might have grabbed a
bottle of non-alcoholic wine
with a heel of whole-wheat bread

Now I haven't really been praying to Jesus
More to the vast mystery
the generic god-spirit-multiverse

because when I talk about Jesus
I get mad at Christians
wonder what the Lord & Savior

has done for me lately
I mean since dying
on a torture device

not quite 2000-years ago
but I am hurting
for that story today

I am hungry to hear someone say
"the Lord be with you"
to rip that whole wheat bread

& to be completely honest
more than the liturgy
prayers or hymns

I am most ravenous for
the material gifts of God
for the people of God

that is right
the calories included in
the body & the blood

so even in my
angry cynical unchurched
deconstructed state

there is something waiting
for me at the table &
the presider invited me

an exiled ex-preacher
backsliding postmodern heretic
heathen but a hungry one

still craving forgiveness
still craving solidarity
still craving community

still needing
mercy & sacrifice
so I tuned-into YouTube church

I even mumbled the creed
but most importantly
I took communion today

JUST ANOTHER DRUG

an aging man of
some significant status
in his former life

said to me in no uncertain
terms at the height of
a conflict regarding another man

that my love for the word
my love for speaking the word
my love for the pulpit

& by that he also meant the office
of preacher & officiant &
every vestment that goes with it

he said for you this is just another drug
he said that to a sober drunk me that
he knew was struggling he said

your vocation & calling are
just another fix to make you feel good
you are addicted to your audience

& any praise that might come
he said that in fewer words &
meant that as an insult

except in my heart I knew at
some base base level it
was entirely unquestionably true

because for the real drunks
anything good & sweet that
we ever chase will one day

turn rotten & sour
will try to kill us
if we let it

i am not right now
feeling sorry for myself
on my pity pot as I write

but all the robes & stoles
& vestments are hanging
in the closet all the

sermons past are sitting
untouched on Google Drive or
some on Soundcloud

now the real pulpit
the real altar is the
compost pile in the back yard

where food rots with
every illusion of power too
as dirty earth is still holy

as it always & should be

UPSIDE DOWN

when your world turns upside down
your friends don't come around no
your friends don't come around
like they used to

check the boxes on the intake form
you say you like yoga like
you say you remember
the day you were born

pastor or clergy not the same as poet
not the same as medicine man
you say it's from God but maybe be honest
true faith is actually admitting that nobody had a plan

spiritual burnout
spiritual bypassing
toxic positivity
spiritual abuse

you have a list & it's getting longer
but somehow on the inside
what doesn't kill you
only makes you stronger

a walking test-case & poster-child
inner scars that you wear like a smile
on the outside just trying to
live before you die

a revolution worthy of an ugly cry
i know you're sober but
why do your eyes make you
look so freaking high

floods & puddles & fires
car crash & blue lights
chain restaurants & late night snacks
hating boundaries when i want my life back

an autumn equinox to kill my summer blues
a concert costume & some Halloween shoes
tired of the don't i need a do do do
might act drunk without a drop of booze

so i'm clocking out & checking in
refuse the cookie-cutter idea of sin
open the doors & let the stranger in
open the cage because the prisoner is kin

build a table & make a feast
call down the angels & ancestors
call out the winds from west & east
refusing the wars bringing the peace

BEING POWERLESS

being powerless
requires so much power

being faithless in gods
is itself an act of faith

walking away from one thing
you are still walking toward someplace else

letting go of one thing
usually requires holding on to something else

being shameless
still kicks in the shame

being nameless
is the greatest name

NON-SPECIFIC THEIST

what is a non-specific theist
to do
not a trinity
not just the whole community
right about now
I could worship
Covid immunity

what is the spiritual
but not religious
to do
now that you know
you can exhale

that Job is just a parable
Noah another parable
Revelation just some good sci-fi

but the waters are still rising
extreme weather but
your micromanager
control freak version
of the divine ain't
got no time

to push water upstream
to suspend the rules of gravity
to black out the sun
gosh darn this rational acceptance
of actual reality ain't much fun

still craving the magic
& the myth
universal love
& the betrayal of a kiss
we still like the stories
the tall tales
is anybody with me

what if I really did let go
the doctrine of original sin
is there any other faith tradition
that is ready to let a
dirty rotten sinner in

IT TAKES MORE FAITH

it takes more faith
to really let go

it takes more faith
to simply say no

it takes more faith
to walk away than to stay

it takes more faith
to accept that barely good enough
is sometimes the best that you can do

CHECK ALL THE BOXES

do i just check all the boxes
buy all the books
listen to all the podcasts
join all the support groups
for the recovering ex-religious

do i just park my ass in
another metal folding chair
where i unload all the pent-up
hurt anger fear anxiety & shame

do i tell you that i have left a cult
am in need of massive
deprogramming

what do i do when every word
the expert said about religious trauma
seems to apply to me

what do i do when i get the text
of extreme relief
laughter & crying why does
so much intensity of living
feel like a part of me is dying

what do i do when i realize
that the churches didn't want
Jesus to be the last & only Christ
& certainly not the last crucified

what do i do when you show me
with your words & your actions
that even you don't believe your

Bibles that you claim to be inerrant
that you cling to like a baby blanket
why are Christians for the most part
such hypocritical bitches

what do i do
i am just over here asking
what do i do when
i am just down here digging a deeper bottom

what do i do when
i am just needing more therapy
more counseling
more relief

what do i do when
i acknowledge that i can't drink over this
what do i do
what the fuck do i do

RELIGION WITHOUT RELIGION

remember when you first
heard that phrase
religionless Christianity &
you are like how does

that work if it all like
the tag spiritual but
not religious just another
bumper sticker t-shirt

relationship not religion
or religion is for the people
avoiding hell & spirituality
is for those of us who have

already been but now i am
staring back through the
headlights the foglights
the hindsight & i get it

even without the MAGA heresies
religion is dead because
we killed it to make a
shrine to its memory

so here we are chasing
those stained-glass ghosts
in our rose-colored glasses
all the while the red flags

of church hurt are invisible
to the doped & drugged &
unhugged why did i always
feel like an outsider or a thug

so today it feels so incredibly
free to simply pull out that rug
but we had to wait way past
intolerable until you had

no other choice
no other options
no other moves
but to leave

DESPERATION NOT VIRTUE

we come to spirituality
from desperation not virtue
i heard the speaker say
or something like that

my journey back to church
started from that holy hunger
of pure desperation in the
rock bottom drunk crawling

back home but then home
was too easy for the prodigal
crawling from the mud to
the pedestal & then like

nothing i got addicted to
virtue to the word teacher
if i am honest i got addicted
to the robes the credentials

the privileges & honors to
preside at the table or at
the grave shoveling dirt on
the coffin looking at my

boots on the ground to make
sure that i am still connected
to my body because the life
of the preacher was always

too surreal for my gathered
files & piles & knicknacks
of suddenly too nice but let
me be honest that virtue never

fit me the robes & stoles aside
i was always more prostrate visions
than professional vestments but
now i am also addicted to the way

my hands felt gripping that old
wooden pulpit looking at the light
cascading in the window or through
the crack in the epic doors of that

old stone church by the river
but for me it was not meant to
last because the more i nuzzled
to virtue the more i muzzled spirit

i knew then that others were not
living up to what we said we meant
what we said we stood for
what we said we were doing

in the later confessions in the
later proclamations of the
last several general assemblies
so when i dig back through

these fading memories my
future was already falling apart
because the addiction to status
started me lying or at least

leaving parts out that i know
i should say so i am not sorry
for the way i spoke up that
got me out the door but

for not speaking up sooner
for black & trans & queer
siblings & for unmarried &
unsure yes for heretics like me

i only regret that an addiction
to virtue over desperation tricked
me into thinking that those boots
were more than dirty sandals

on the dirty feet of a broken man
who still needs that gentle Jesus
to wash those feet to forget my
sins to hold my sore swollen hand

WHAT DOES IT MEAN

social justice what does
that even mean Biblical justice
vindictive justice restorative justice
just words sprayed all over this screen

since i am already being honest
telling you what i really think
i am actually not very good at forgiveness
or forgetting so if i had stayed in a Christian

church where no matter how much history or
PhD-level interpretation we show you
you continue to weaponize your religion
against women & immigrants & Muslims &

queers i would one day snap
you see i suppose that is exactly
what happened i broke into pieces
like a weary decaying rubberband

stretched too many times now i am simply
beside myself with a holy rage that is right
if i had stayed in your church i would have gone
all Detroit on you i would have gone all Old Testament

if i stayed in church i would have turned
over tables not as a metaphor no i would
have joined the indigenous of Canada &
the metal heads of Europe & i would have

gone to the store & got my gas & my matches
& we would have taken revenge against you
for all the dead fags & closeted dykes & murdered trans
for all the indigenous of this very land where

you built that building if i had stayed i would
have gone all Mark Driscoll book of Revelation
on your crackerjack hypocrisy & i would have
just set the whole place on fire as justice

Jesus incorporated trademark commodity Jesus
is an enemy of Jesus in the guise of the poor
the church is an enemy of the church
we are all enemies of ourselves

see now they are preaching restorative justice
for abusers for rapists for January 6 rioters
they are all like forgiveness & grace man for
the ancestors who bought & sold other humans

so i left church in order to save my spirit from itself
i left church to save love from love
i left church to save my soul from seeing you every
Sunday with the permanent frown on your face

because i was starting to believe all that hellfire shit
& i was all but ready to turn it back on every single
racist sexist fascist nationalist Christian in America
so i left church & i am not sure i can ever come back

because love itself
is more important than
love as indoctrination in this
here flag-waving Jesus nation

NOT WRONG NOT RIGHT

i am not wrong but i am definitely not right
i might sleep nine hours or be up all night
i am not not good but i might be sometimes bad
i am everything gushing on the counselor's pad

we are all victims all perpetrators despite
our intention to keep the creed harm none
we are the many we are the some we are
the ninety-nine & we are the one

do you as you will when just living with
yourself is the toughest pill to swallow
anticipating the repercussions when cancel
culture catches up & leaves your heart hollow

time to cancel myself because this honesty is too much
is making me tired as my soul drags on the ground
life is wandering for joy for beauty for truth but
then you end up another ragged stray left at the pound

is it any wonder we went
running for the church doors
sins dripping like honey
like sweat from all the pores

you were gone but you never left
this mystery is strange like that
you thought you had it figured out
but it was never this never that

LITERALISM

so the Bible is literal one hundred
percent factual true every single word
without exception & anyone who
proposes a single nuance or tweak

is simply a faithless heathen without
recourse & probably a backsliding
heretic sending others to hell so i
get it i see you so i open my Bible

to the Gospel according to Saint
Matthew chapter twenty five & there
is this super sticky forever chunky
passage where the text says that the

poor & prisoner & hungry & thirsty
& sick are actual Jesus said with such
empathy & such impact it is said that
the poor & prisoner are all that in the

flesh & when some random so-called
progressive Christian pulls out that passage
to talk about the unhoused or jailbirds or addicts
or bums or the Covid wing it's all like no no no

no that is not what my white Jesus meant
how dare your works righteousness shame me
with all that expectation that we actually do
what the text says so instead of the savior

with skin on walking the streets of your city
with his beggar's bucket & you are like hell no
we worship money & America & flags &
Trump & all you poor addicted bums can just

go & you know what rhymes with bucket
so instead of an embodied Lord in great need
that we can meet that we can help you tell
us to stop getting brainwashed by Biden

or stop confessing actual sins like our collective
debt to every descendent of every enslaved
African our debt to every surviving indigenous
trapped on reservations tell them how your

free market climate catastrophe endless war
is the chosen nation because i missed that part
in the text that i have walked away from with
such a bitter tortured broken heart full stop

CHURCH PROBLEMS

1.

you must have been right with God
he said to me as we cleaned up the debris
from the tornado that swept through
our community in March 2020

now wait what was that young child
that died or any of the other
victims for whom trees were planted
not far from my house

were they wrong with God
because that is the part i don't
get about your meteorological Lord
of floods & extreme weather

because you know that
these rains these floods
these tornados
these hurricanes are

actually more likely connected
with how wrong we are with
mama earth than how right or
wrong we are with the disembodied

sky god who would never just
randomly kill children oh wait
hold on there is actually an entire book
where that is exactly what God does

2.

if you had not been dancing
with the hippies & the feminists
& the half-naked weirdos who
took a bath in rainbow glitter

if you had not been camping
with them for three days &
using a porta-shitter instead of
staying home if you had not

been listening to all that loud
music watching all those crazy
light shows if you had not been
paying good money to bring

that festival to our community
well then just maybe just maybe
that tree would not have fallen
on your house okay fine

so God sent that lightning to
hit that tree to fall on my house
to break my roof to destroy my
belongings with rain & soggy insulation

because i love rock-n-roll & like to
go to festivals now we suspect
you were joking just fucking
with me actually in your own

paternalistic redneck manner
but damn bruh i got to wonder
about this God who is allegedly
so good still all the time having

such a problem with dancing
women or rock-n-roll because
that dude kind of sounds like
a jerk who needs a hug & a snack

3.

we were so naive so happy
so in love so enthusiastic so
we wanted to bring music &
candles & potluck & college kids

to brighten up that space on
sunday night so we set out
to make a plan to make a flier
to share on social media that

we were having an informal
inclusive supper church &
we decided to invite everyone
it was going to be so perfect

now because of our energy or
maybe my "emergent church"
vocabulary or perhaps it really
was the candles that is it

the candles now because of
that the elders sent spies &
here we thought you were being
friendly but you were just

hanging out to prove it
really was the devil & not
Jesus who had inspired us
to bake such good bread

to make such good food
to share so much love
to sing so many songs
because yeah we

sat in a circle instead of
neat rows & wait for it
we had candles yep that
must be evil for sure

4.

why don't you come by
the house the single widow
said to me & i immediately
felt like something was off

why don't you call me
why don't you pay attention to me
why don't you do it this way
like the last pastor did

we need to talk she said
every time she called me
to bitch & complain which
began to happen with

increasing frequency because
she needed to tell me
everything that i was
doing poorly now don't

get me wrong i know
i was new i know i was
learning i know all these things
but they weren't even paying

a salary just a stipend
i still had another job now
you are taking over my
life ending my privacy

messing with my marriage
because i have not one
not two but three needy
older single females asking

me everything & then some
can't catch my breath
can't catch a break so
now you say why don't

you provide pastoral counseling
keeping in mind that there
was no particular drama or trauma
or crisis that had been explained

to me it was simply years of
unmanaged unprocessed
family systems & codependency
& abusive husbands that are

now dead by which you can see
this green preacher is in way
way way over his head but
this is what i said or tried to say

i don't provide counseling
because i am not a counselor
y'all hired me as a preacher
you liked that i'm an English teacher

my job is to interpret these texts
but actually what you really
wanted needed was a friend
whose free time was without end

5.

it still breaks my heart to think
how it all went crazy when we
left town for two Sundays for
vacation to Colorado then New York

in the dead of winter we both
ended up getting sick inside
a bomb cyclone stuck in our room
outside a frozen Broadway

Times Square just sat & waited then we
came home to discover the news
the plots the crazy phone calls
the gossip it was gathering against me

somewhere around that time we
attended the women's march in Nashville
it was what just a year into Trump so
we found ourselves in the streets

believe women
support victims
stop grabbing our
you know the word

& now there were more
phone calls because we can't
have a preacher who is
part of the resistance

they even called
the denomination office
to register this complaint
because this is rural Tennessee

oh & then there was the Sunday
after i marched in Murfreesboro
against Charlottesville part two
called white lives matter

she said to me to my face she
understands why they were
marching for whites because our
society only helps black people &

we just aren't doing enough
to support our white youth
& you just sit there on your
hands wanting to yank

your tongue out of your mouth
your heart out of your chest
it's not like the made-for-Netflix
series you thought you were

living where the well-meaning
lefty yankee pastor goes to a country
church to support the people where they
are at & maybe just maybe help

them along to seeing the world
a little less harshly but no
not even their God could heal them
or convince them no not at all

to not be so damaged
not be so messed up
to not be so mean
they just don't teach you

about any of this in divinity school
& despite the national denomination's
progressive inclinations we simply
don't have the resources to

support churches like that
in the deep red heart of
the MAGA nation where
the myth of the purple church

is such a stupid idea
such a waste of my time
such a hurtful retrogressive
lying lie

we don't read the same books
we don't watch the same channels
we don't believe the same things
Apostles Creed or Lord's Prayer aside

with the church in America today
it is not even the same Jesus
it is not the same God &
i am not the insane guy

for explaining
this
as it
actually is

6.

now all of this is not even the worst part
the worst part is
the abuser the groomer
the greedy narcissist

who after months of lying & abuse
tried to get himself off the hook
by saying some such bullshit like
we only kissed

maybe you weren't there
maybe you don't care
but the trauma is real
& so much well-meaning

just get over it
just move on
just let it go
okay fine but it's not

until i do the work
not until i tell the truth
not until i purge myself
of all the shame that

still creeps up to attack me
from deep deep deep
on the inside where
the heart lives

7.

it was a text message
why is it always a text
that came so late at night
here i was miles & miles away

why are they calling a meeting
an emergency meeting
for all the deacons & elders
i don't want to go the text message said

text messages turned to phone calls
turned to rumors
turned to speculation
almost immediately

we got swept up in the drama
we got swept up in the lies
why is my body joining delusion
another text message of endless confusion

8.

thank you for what you are
going to do this week she
said through that permanent
frown but i don't think

we realized this
was one of the last real
conversations that we would
ever have because going to

that meeting was the first
of several steps of seeing
the veil lifted from my eyes
of seeing through your lies

but you didn't stop
messaging me you didn't
stop agreeing to meet with me
even though it violated the

terms of your exclusion
from ordered ministry
during the investigation
preceding the charges

you were meeting with lots
of people even taking
command of the board
of elders because you

were going to beat this
thing back where you broke
some very serious rules
by breaking more rules

because the rules just
don't apply to powerful
white male narcissists
& our denial will help us

bypass countless boundaries
wait what you were supposed to
respect boundaries as a
part of your vows that

just didn't come as part
of your career as a
groomer predator
exploiter pastor cheat

9.

you got the call on a Friday night
the charges had been brought
you were angry & confused but
most of all completely distraught

there is no way that all these people
that you trusted that you know really cared
would have dared to take this step
based on the fabricated lies he shared

unless maybe
the accusations were true
now what
are we going to do

when you went to the meeting the next day
you walked around in a surreal haze
are these churches ever the right place for
wild unkempt desires for unsafe space

all around you the world unraveled
you didn't really need the judge or his gavel
all those long car trips to this very meeting
different sanctuaries many miles traveled

it was on those endless rides there or back
he professed that this was the best group of
elders & preachers & when exactly did
that idea fall completely off the tracks

where his former friends all got the blame
where his former mentors paid for the shame
where a clear-cut process he made into a game
where the real people hurt all have names

they had a free book table next to all the snacks
you were supposed to be back upstairs with
a name badge & an electronic copy of the packet
but this discarded library called out to you fast

you were not ready to own the skeletons of your past
not ready to admit that you are not that different
just relieved by years in recovery of active actions
now you no longer betrayed everything in your values

like when you were wasted not just on booze but on bending
the truth so now that this new case was pending
you picked up that book & slipped it in your bag
mumbling to a friend you won't believe this

it was such an incredible drag but we were stuck up
in it without a clear idea of what is true but you
were starting to see & it twisted you all around
but that is what you get when in the words or friendship

of a leader is where all your self-worth & identity
can be found so there you are just sitting through
the day not sure how you can go along not sure
how you can still play the ally & advocate to someone

who is so sure they have to fight fight fight & for this
for how many months did this drama keep you
up all night until you finally admitted that you
were his victim too not just you but everyone who

was in that room that Saturday morning from
across the region & everyone in that sweet church
the next day when his defenders passed that hat
to pay for his lawyers thousands raised just like that

the book was called *Sex & the Spiritual Teacher* &
slowly you learned how the predator is also the preacher
we humans when consumed by enlightened delusions like
power as lust we become such crazy crazy hurtful creatures

NOT THE FIELD THAT RUMI SPOKE OF

i am sorry that these are mostly not poems
that take us to the field that Rumi spoke of
to touch the resurrected flesh that Thomas
touched or holding hands & hoisting

wildflowers above all our heads because
that would be so much more satisfying
than this stuck in the muck meaningless
meaning of folks floundering for purpose

see i was there with you when we won
when we believed that justice had been done
folks were listening & folks believed that
a collective good was better than a selfish

need & from that moment of catharsis so
many were internally freed but the stay
was only temporary a technicality simmered
legality behind the doors of private emails

something sneaky still percolated to undo
four years of accountability four years of
strange healing & somehow confused i
stumble today only a borrower of your side

of the story where some of these church people
turned out to be not hateful not hypocrites
hopeful purveyors of believing victims of
honoring women & oh how i wish we just hit

the pause button that winter day a little big longer
to take too many gasps or gulps of air but
what we are seeing isn't really ever crawling to
fair & maybe i just forgive & forget it all

trust me i am working on it & it sucks that
my bumbling stumbling version is so partial
a perspective that the glimpses of reconciliation
have faded in the same drawer where i think

i keep a printed copy of the final decision so
when i sat on that colleague's porch was it late
winter or early spring i was never ready for such
smug derision i could not predict the consequence

of every cosmic collision but i still believe that
no matter how chaotic or confused just beneath
this smile that a magnetic compass of love will
still guide me past past past that Rumi field even

past past past that Thomas touch to a place where
everything is always way too much but something
maybe just another taste of paradise is barely but
sufficiently so much perhaps even just enough

DON'T WANT TO BE BETTER

sometimes i just don't want to be better
I don't want to be right
just dance all night
I don't want to get worse
but I don't want to get well
holier than thou is just
another kind of hell

I don't want to flatline
into numb nothingness
I have learned to love all the mess
like I love all the memes

this one is for all my
fellow neurodivergents
you might know what I mean
what did it say

too many tabs on the computer
too much laundry on the floor
too much garbage in the backseat of the car
too many times being late for everything

when I was a kid
I liked to close my eyes
press my hands on the lids
then look at the light
& wait for the spirals
sometimes I would make
my feet fall asleep on purpose
because I want to feel
the pins & needles &

like right now I am okay with
the tentacles of a real
messy dirty broken life

you don't really know or care
that I have been
born again & again
baptized by the water
been washed in the blood
have cleansed my chakras
have done all the mindfulness meditation
have attended your overpriced
shamanic training
have drank the mushroom tea
swallowed everything but the kool aid
that says some Instagram-curated
perfection is what we needed in
the first place or the last place
just give me the guitar solos
that might melt my face

I have tried booze & religion
abstinence & drugs
walking & dancing
yoga & vegetarianism
raw garlic or herb tea
self-help books on Audible
self-help books on Kindle
getting advice from
strangers in the self-help
aisle at McKays tried
getting up early
staying up late
writing in my journal every day

forgive me for being willing yet
for a million more modalities
as long I get to keep my
critique of the principalities

yes forgive me for being unsure
of another step after the 12
another mental hack to try
but I will keep trying everything
until the day that I die

just get me out of my bed
just get me out of my head
even into outer space is
it any wonder we are the types
to self-medicate because we
cannot successfully smash
the state of affairs that doesn't
care but yet misdiagnosed
overprescribed
on a pharmaceutical dare

we are getting high while
the planet is dying
when we say we are fine
we are always lying
why are we only honest
when we are crying
not just low hum whimpering
but full on bawling
I mean snot slinging
out of key singing
happy rage bringing

I don't want a fix
not even a cure
just plant some more
flowers in this here
pile of manure

SPIRIT IS REALITY

not a big fan of karma
not even sure about grace
just learning to never be one
who thinks they can tell others their place

all these abstract concepts
to which we pledge our lives
I just want to pledge life to the living
maybe spirit is just reality in disguise

I always imagined that
not believing would require
more faith than belief
not saying I am an atheist

not saying that we understand
what is the underlying everything
that we see right in front of our face
for some of us this is terrifying

for some of us this is exhilarating
some don't have time for
all this contemplating but with me
I don't even know which is the case

OCTOBER DAYS

the clouds are rolling in with the
leaves rustling now & it suddenly finally
feels like fall with just a few October
days left to dance in the darkening

i am acutely aware of approaching
Halloween of All Saints All Souls all
that this season is now we have our
shelf for the ancestors we have our

pumpkins gourds candy & skulls &
i have playlists & songs prepared to
share with solemn not so spooky but
deeply spiritual connection to these

here hills these here hollers these
graveyards or cemeteries these
memories of the first time i sat on
a straw bale as a bench around a

bonfire around a folk song these
haunted hills & hollers are part of
me have been for 25 years since
i settled in just down the way i didn't

stay in one place but i chose this
place of Cherokee land this place
of hunters & hippies of granola
meets good-ol-boy or something

like that now it says in some other
poems that i am leaving church that
i am done with one kind of institution
but if i am true to my inner notion there

is all kinds of backwood old time
religion that we still respect that we
still practice that is potluck hospitality
that is healing remedies that is crafty

calming creative full moon crazy i will
never get lazy for chasing the magic that is
reality if we are open to it in the
changing seasons & the spirits they bring

LIFE PHILOSOPHY

don't know my Plato from Plotinus
my Heidegger from Hegel
because I am not as well-read as you think
but my philosophy is life

so give me Dorothy Day or David Graeber
some John Muir or Emma Goldman
some homeless-loving treehugging anarchist
you know what I mean

love your neighbor
do what you will
harm-reduction self-care
DIY or die

we remember ACT-UP & Food Not Bombs
reclaim the Test Site & Redwood Summer
that we are still battling the same old stuff
could feel like such a bummer

but it doesn't it won't it can't because
we won't let them have our joy
so much more powerful when together
we believe in freedom & never give up

so overcomplicated & misunderstood that
I keep it simple
stay sober & keep some single dollars
to tip every busker or panhandler that I see

I went to see some punk rock last night
it's been too long
danced like crazy
knew just a few of the songs

shook my bones
raised my fist
when was the last time that
you felt like this

maybe such a long-haired
older cat could feel like
he didn't belong but thoughts
like that would be so wrong

we get high on coffee in the day
relax with herb tea at night
we go to battle with hope & love
don't have to show up at every fight

but the fight of our lives
is human survival
planetary survival
no more denial

just seeking that inner teacher
believe that inner truth
give some radical empathy
to this former preacher

CHRISTMAS AMONG THE DECONSTRUCTED

Christmas among
the deconstructed
no stranger to longing
not a bucket of faith
to fill a backpack of doubt

but who doesn't want
to go chasing magic
who doesn't hunger
for candles when the
lights get turned down

my whole being
responds to Silent Night
or Brightest & Best or
Hark Some Herald Angels Sing
even if I don't want a king

we crave that messy abundance
of familiar & uncomfortable &
stained glass memories that
shatter into refracted revolutions
that always welcome refugees

my lineage is broken & unbroken
as twisted as these Mt. Tamalpais trees
or eating spicy curries close
to midnight at a North Beach eatery
something in the song still beckons

& begs to sing carols to the deconstructed
hymns to the enchanted & exiled
prophetic poems to light the fires
of resistance & the unlearning yet
childlike attraction to the holy night

CHASING CAROLS

complicated & confusing
but chasing carols still
for the place that the song
lands in my chest
opens up the waterfalls of feeling

of course we pick & choose
unlimited compassion
& uplifting the poor
not just as symbols
but embodied solidarity

so we forever tap
our lineage of
mystics & revolutionaries
without apologies
ignoring toxic theologies

chasing carols & communities from
the manger from the margins
from the bottom from the barn
to the beautiful at the barricades
that is the mystery where the work begins

PAPER JESUS

paper Jesus
words on a bulletin
manger made of ink
these minds after divinity
will we use them to think?

paper Jesus
all the verses in a book
but at the bottom of our days
we still don't give the
stranger a second look

paper Jesus
watched as we forgot or burned
others' books smoldering in a pile
the Bible remains unopened they
like the name of Jesus but not his style
paper Jesus
the time of year to
get out your most beautiful songs
but what would be even better for those
crusaders to take back all the wrongs

done in the name of
paper Jesus

paper Jesus
is it just a story
with some parts filled with love
but the other parts
are much more gory

paper Jesus
just let it go because all
this theology is too much to bear
just show me a remnant of followers who
do more than just pretend to care

paper Jesus
still see you in the jails
still see you on the freeway flyin a sign
but a houseless savior cannot stop a
religion that is hell-bent on lyin

paper Jesus
the only contract that was asked
was to love one another
but we refuse to love our siblings
much less the ones perceived as other

paper Jesus
if your heart is real it is breaking with mine
hoping you would just jump off the page
to cast out the demons of this age &
show us that you are more

than just a
paper Jesus

NOW AUTHENTICITY

now authenticity is just another alcoholism
to discern your calling is just another crack
falling asleep while watching a show
then wide awake when I am
trying to doze just
flat on my back

now I need a deconstruction
from my deconstruction
what addict doesn't want a drug
to cure them from drugs

now this world of inappropriate breaking boundaries
we cannot even ask for hugs not drugs & we are mostly okay
with this because to be honest some folks
we don't want to hug but we still need one

now the spiritual has been stolen by the spirituality of theft
when you finish one really good book you can never
find the next one of the proper mental heft
oh the books that would cure me from always reading
the true heartache that might fix me from always needing

now always so powerless over the
world's imperfections doesn't mean
just gobble cruelty & cynicism like a confection
every day another opportunity for correction
understand the problem but refuse protection
stay too busy for even a moment of reflection

now the day is so drab that we decorate with
decorations for our demoralized dreary yet
all kinds of decorations cannot stop the bottom we face
the duty of denial facing the addiction of delight
then just praying to make it through the night

now without the perfect real without the
imperfect truth
now will you
buy this potion
this pill
this trip
will you step into the booth
like Pilate we ask what is truth

now we are all just carnival barkers
at the festival of the end times
where we cannot
find our path
but will always find rhymes

now no solution
no ideology
no mantra
no absolute truth
no party
no church
no magical new age
no guru
no god
without grace
when even goodness
has been weaponized
yet we refuse the
saving mask on
our human face

now you admit it
that it was always a game
a narrative or
performance where
the characters change
but the broken bottom
for lovers & liars will
always remain the same

now please don't mistake this rant
for grim grumpy despair
I will still dance the dance
still spin in circles at the fair
love without looking back
walk forward as if I didn't care

but don't accept the invitation to
a spiritual path without seeing it
as a dare to lose everything
to sacrifice security in all its forms
to accept the potential suffering
from which all wisdom is born

SAYINGS THAT DRIVE ME CRAZY Nº1

"You are not a human having a spiritual experience,
you are a spirit having a human experience"

uh
no
this humanness
this earthiness
this home
this interaction between bodies
consciousness
& the material plane
for all their failures
flaws
uncomfortable diversities
is our reality right now
right now is all we have

perhaps the veil will be punctured to
show me different but until then
such ghoulish gnostic gibberish
is just one more layer
to our body blaming
body shaming
reality
gaming escape
from what
to what
you don't even know
my toes are in the soil
here i am planted
here is where we grow

the fully human body is where the spirit lives

PATH BEFORE ME

the path before me
just another open window
just the hungry mouth
of the gaping sky

the path ahead as I escape religion
as I run from the pulpit through the doors
onto the gravel street & straight to
the mountains or the creek

here we go down this path
with a pack of grief & lots of grub
as many snacks as we can pack
into this hobo satchel

every seeker is a friend to these
tracks these weeds that sky
from the day we are born
until the day we die

I cannot really retrace my steps
even as I want to reread books
got too many words but
forgot all the hooks

but the walls of church are
crumbling behind me the death
of God or faith or what I don't know
because Jesus is still a rebel

to whom I might listen as I listen
to the water keepers & earth defenders
as I listen to the workers organizing &
the junkies getting clean & drunks getting dry

& the people flying signs or trespassing in tents or
writing codes with their misconduct
to explode the myths with new ones
we write new stories unravel old fabric to stitch new

still a devotional distraction & powerless surrender
to immersion in the radical mystery
seek to understand new weird things
as much as old weird history

i am grateful to be lost again
unfound from straightjackets of salvation &
discourses on damnation that defy or deny
this sacred reality of nondual liberation

BEYOND

beyond syncretic
beyond new age
beyond interfaith
beyond interspiritual

beyond a vague
universalism to be
part of a particular
visionary universe

animated & always
asking us to show up
inside these
interstellar skins

stardust primates
with wild brains
such beautiful bodies
given dawn

who are you beatnik Buddhist
psychedelic abstinent
sober insanity
anarchist Christian

dancing dervish
polymorphous polyphony
all the monks are singing
the stand-up comics getting high

we take a vow to
an inner truth
an outer wisdom
forever unveiled ghost

GOD IS SUCH A SHOWOFF

it is ridiculous & absurd to be so obsessed
with religion & theology when the galaxy
keeps knocking you over with the rustled breeze
not sure the saints were also thus rattled or coddled

to grab their knees under a bucket of crying
every week a midlife crisis every week
more of your stupid ego dying but get out
on the trail to suckle on waterfalls because

God is such a damn showoff isn't She &
somehow you got to be an earthling with
a consciousness & a taste for fungus &
moss & trees that talk louder than Bibles

about that green man Jesus or that witchy
goddess Mary or any of them other avatars
or deities getting down to the roots to
fondle rotten leaves & speak howling gibberish

call me vulnerable & sensitive in the extreme
more available to spiritual influence than a
thousand Rumi or Mary Oliver quotes for
your next Instagram meme do you spot a

theme for the waking rest of this human dream
where we give more than a damn about planetary
survival transform a planet filled with lies about property
because all currency is crypto is made up is toxic

so let's declare amnesty get past transactional exchange to
cancel debts with generational change to generosity unleashed
like the Diggers were right yes the mystics were onto
something which is finally ready for everything & anything

RIDING WITH MERTON

I'm riding shotgun in Kentucky with Merton
howling in the desert with Richard Rohr
sick to my guts from all their published wisdom
as my tired ass falls down through another trap door

been reaching rock bottoms since back in the day
sun on my face dirt on my shoes
hungry heart cannot keep pace with busy brain
broken from much more than booze

look look gotta keep look looking
sang the song about lost & found blindness & sight
but some days you get so mad at the slogans or
mad at yourself just wanna make it through the night

some things worse than another bottom would
not be feeling the gravel & glass on that tired ass
no matter how many times you remind yourself that
in this life of lessons more failure is the only way to pass

WINDOW IN MY HEAD

there is a window
in the back of my head
that opens during yoga class

I don't remember
what pose just that
I was lying on my back

with the opening into trees
with leaves like flames
branches like brains

even though the teacher
said to let go or
focus on the breath

I was talking to the trees
& with a gust of summer breeze
those green flames started flapping

hands started clapping
my siblings with their roots
drinking soul in the soil

declared their family ties
to my aches & past lies
just another rooted being

with pink hairy bark
with hunger for the stars at night
never fear the dark

like Casey once sang
I like to walk at night
these woods for me hold no fright

my only fear is that
one day these
trees won't be here

any longer

NATURE POEMS

I was so stupid for rejecting you for so long
as great but something boring

for old people on bird walks
I am those old people now

overstimulation suffer me screen
lace up these shoes give me green

deep green like green man or Hildegard
chants of wild nature mystics

because as I sit & weep in the
bottom of a dry creek bed I am

better because there I spoke to
a tiny frog & a black butterfly

the Goddess is not shy about
showing her mushrooms & moss

so we shake off the world
of shout & shame to shudder

instead in gratitude for the
boring quiet bursting gust

of old-school romantic tree-intoxicated
dharma bum hobo nature poems

JESUS LOST TOO

Jesus lost his lawsuit too
Jesus never had his day in court
the system isn't set up to woo you
just wait you'll see how they do you

Herod Pilate Calvary or the
middle district of Tennessee
institutions set up in perpetuity
don't even say that they are temporary

petition "The Man" to make right
the man's wrongs but don't you know
ain't nobody with power wants
to listen to that song

the boss says work
the boss says when
the boss is a jerk
like God in the Garden of Eden

groveling for justice from
the kings of injustice
lawyers act like outlaws
outlaws hide from cops

please did you
get the memo
about who is on the bottom
& who is on the top

you want some kind of power
believe that your no means no
but they control the levers
of when you stay or when you go

some colleagues & friends don't care
ignore your emails won't take your call
shocked when someone else might say
do you even work here at all

we want to join a union
we want to organize & fight
but when the boss keeps beating you back
can't even sleep through the night

here when the powerless are right
know that the powerful are wrong
the world looks the other way
time to cut the chains & hum a different song

THE GLORY OF THE LORD

flying on the slick hilly roads
in a silver Prius we are shocked
to bliss by the misty beauty of fall

bold oranges or muted browns
brilliant reds or screaming yellows
the shower of death is glorious color

everywhere the evidence of the living dying
cosmic god of the long time
longer than forever old as dirt holy

amid the rolling roads of rural autumn
somebody has nailed a plastic sign
to a sacred tree declaring the glory of the Lord

as if in the midst of the amazing fire of autumn
on a long drive on a rainy sunday afternoon
we need a plastic sign to tell us the glory of God

when Her natural evidence is
constantly singing to the
souls inside our eyes

HERE FOR IT

like Han Solo
in episode 7
saying of the Force
it is all true
just like that
I am here for it
all of it

for hocus pocus & mumbo jumbo
for magic & sober medicine
for prayer & meditation
for speaking in tongues & laying on hands
for Tarot cards & Bible verses
for Aloha & Shalom
for peace be with you & Namaste
for Jesus Christ & Gautama Buddha
for love your neighbor & love yourself
for nonviolence & nonattachment
for powerlessness & higher powers
for theology & geology
for father God & mother Goddess
for pronouns & proper nouns
for we & us
for they & them
for How It Works & Easy Does It
for poetry & rock-n-roll
for fresh-baked bread & non-alcoholic wine
for unconditional grace & unlimited gravity
for the beautiful & the good
for mythopoetic & liturgical
for naive wonder & the wheel of the year
for stained glass & rose-colored glasses

for rainbows & unicorns
for letting go & letting God
for surrender & surrender again
for the end of weeping & my cup runneth over

& if I am honest I am also here
for desperation & despair
for disillusion & dry spells
but sometimes I can't write
poetry about these

I am here for the scabs on my knees
for crawling & praying to
satisfy human needs

I MIGHT STILL BE A CHRISTIAN

about a year ago I started
calling myself "Christian-adjacent"

some of my friends were like
"I have no idea what that means"

I don't know what it means either but
I could say the same for Christianity itself

yet somehow I felt this tug to distance myself
from all the creeds & crusty old doctrines

not to mention all the cranky judgers
at church with all their petty agendas

even if I was still endlessly wrestling
with the love-talk & the cross

in Anne Lamott's conversion narrative in
Traveling Mercies she talks about her lineage

with parents who were secular hipsters
with friends who were stoned hippies

California leftists all of them & with such a crowd
calling yourself a Christian is just plain awkward

she resisted at first the call that Jesus placed on her
because frankly it wasn't cool & who would believe her

I think I have resembled Anne Lamott my
entire adult life but in this regard especially

I still remember when Sunfrog
got sober he encountered an illuminated

Jesus & joined AA &
some friends just frankly thought I was joking or

maybe needing medication
more than revelation

earlier this summer I saw that a favorite religious author
Brian McLaren was making the podcast circuit again

oh—he must be peddling a new book
this one is called *Do I Stay Christian?*

& deep inside my body my spirit-brain was
clamoring "why are you asking that now"

I already deconstructed—don't you read my blog?
I already left religion—sort of & a second time

but of course we all know why he was asking it now
because MAGA Trumpists tried to chase us all

out of church if not out of Tennessee or
the south if not out of America entirely

but more importantly there is this utterly
annoying absolutely intoxicating possibly invented

maybe completely made-up story of Jesus that keeps
creeping back into my thoughts without my consent

come on now you might know what I am talking about the
Holy Spirit has no boundaries or respect for my agnostic side

prefers not to take "no" for answer when
you already said "yes" a hundred times before

so here we are in my monthly weekly daily midlife
existential crisis where I admit the godawful truth

that I cannot live with church &
I cannot live without it &

besides you may think I'm a backsliding heretic
but whoever heard of anyone being unbaptized

I could not live without God even if I tried
yes because God is as real as life itself is &

like Ashley Cleveland sang
"I Need Jesus" & there's more:

as a retired pastor & I agreed on a phone call that
while organized religion may be a net bad in the world

it has still been a net good in our lives even if it is
just some approximation of faith that some

Christian scholars once dubbed "therapeutic deism"
I frankly prefer some framework of the divine

in my life rather than not & because the religion
of my lineage & of my youth feels radically more

authentic than any of the delicious alternatives
that I have explored & frankly perhaps I understand

what some studies say:
"Participating in spiritual practices may be

a protective factor for a range
of health & well-being outcomes"

I have to admit not just my genuine interspirituality but
that the Christianity at the core of my being speaks to me

in the voice of Jesus in the voice of scripture in the voice
of protesters & in the broken bread & juice or wine & even

in the voice of the radical
theologians who have come before

& I also have to admit: I love the brimming yumminess of the
Whitmanian multitudes spilling over the edges of our existence

so that I can include
Buddha & Laozi & tree spirits &

fairies & unicorns & The Force
& Tarot Cards & the I-Ching

& sacred Mama Earth & mutual aid & anarchism
& my beloved Unitarian Universalists even as

I walk this undeniable Jesus path with all its
consequences of crosses & enemy love

So like the shock of the first cup of coffee before the
first light of dawn I have to admit it this morning that

I might still be a Christian

GOOD TROUBLE

I have a confession
to make about all
that "good trouble"
that I was in
not that long ago

it wasn't that good
not for me

it wasn't that good
while I was going through it
a downpour of
anxiety & shame & self-doubt

maybe it would have
been good when I was younger
crazier stronger

when I was younger
I climbed fences
trespassed
pretended to be dead
while lying in the street
blocking traffic
taunting cops

but not now
I feel too old
for this revolution
that we are always losing
& I actually liked these jobs
that I seemed bent on losing

I didn't count it but joy
all this internal suffering
& don't even get me
started about the patience
this was supposed to produce
at least that is what the
good book told me

for a season I even stopped praying
even if I mouthed all the words
at the end of the 12-step meeting

maybe I have learned & grown
my counselor says now I have perspective
even authentic gratitude
but I don't think I have patience
or joy when I am deep in it
going through the difficult situation
does not feel much like liberation

& please don't let this be
about another persecuted white dude
arguing with another white dude
about race & class & privilege

I understand why some white folks
hate the "woke" white people &
I guess I am one of the woke ones

but freedom only comes when
I am one of the broken ones

when my deconstruction
walks directly into a brick wall
& bounces from a rock bottom
straight into the arms of Jesus

I am done with my own abstractions
& finished with my platitudes
just slinging snot & singing old gospel songs
falling to my knees & bawling tired ugly cry
& my sister is a black preacher is laying on the hands
casting out the demons & building a hedge

once again I have walked to the edge
& I can hear the angels sing in a small
modest African-American church not
five minutes from my house in a
neighborhood called the West End

& the church shares a parking lot with
a bar & grill & is just off the highway
in the working-class industrial part of
town where there are other churches
& barber shops & restaurants where
Spanish is spoken & I am thinking of Anne Lamott
getting drawn like a magnet to the black church
by the flea market in Marin, California

when there was no place left to go because she
like me is just another lost hippie leftist alcoholic
who needs the soulful gospel music & the tender loving
arms of Christ to save her from herself

ours is a big tent becoming a bigger tent
I still need my daily doses of yoga & coffee
& dancing like you ain't watching always dancing
& my vegetarian food & my long hikes
with theology podcasts when it's not new age
treehugger podcasts & all rolled up in all of it
is the voice that says you are my beloved child

IRRESISTIBLE NONVIOLENCE
JESUS INTOXICATION

at an extremely young age
I met the irresistible
face-painted rabbi
the dancing prophet
the wine-spilling friend

from the folk songs
to the sermons to
the people with guitars & beards
ripping the crust of bread to
dip in the chalice of juice

I might have known the word
though didn't understand
"hippy" just yet
but the hair was everywhere
the cut-off jeans
they say it's a vibe

the vibe was inside me
part of my formation
lying in the bunk
at summer camp
feeling what I imagine was
meditation just to feel
the energy surrounding us

are you there God
the humming vibrations
just filled the room
electric energy long before
the first jolt of intoxication
but like Miley & Noah sing
I got so high that
I saw Jesus

as irresistible & intoxicating
as the mystical met me
in my adolescent mess
there was more
it was always inclusive
always antiwar
always for the the poor
always more
so when they knock
we always open the door

the connection between
church & nonviolence
between the upside-down kingdom
& the socialist commons
were so incontrovertible
& so real that it still
spins & spits me to see
their macho god of hate
in the Jesus place
their god of war
their god of hate

our current impasse
inspires us in
desperation & determination
to apply doctrine to the deed
to ask theodicy or theology
to show us a way out
but there's so much just
in the story that requires

recitation more than interpretation
Jesus said what Jesus said

Jesus did what Jesus did
& did it all for love
so I see the radical sacrifice of
radical peace & radical powerlessness
where they see
mechanical manipulation of
substitutionary atonement &
it only gets worse from there

can't we just apply
"Damned for All Time" &
"Blood Money" from
Jesus Christ Superstar
to a video about all
the gun manufacturers
all the bomb factories
all these nuclear war pimps
& slaves to the gods of war
war & more war
anyone can buy a
killing machine at
the local store

would you still follow Jesus
should you learn that
his Daddy isn't the
megalomania monster that
you made him
would you still stand
at the feet of the cross
to sing were you there
were you there

every martyr gets
manipulated into every
outward projection
every monstrous hatred
an alienated distortion
from the God of love
but still we seek
the inner mysteries
the collective festival
the communal feast
contemplation in the
service of liberation
in this we love
the one who loved us
forever broken from
your terror code
hallelujah amen

P.S.
I could list all the authors
in my anarchist pacifist
Christian lineage but
I'm not sure it
would matter at this late hour
of short arguments made
for Twitter or TikTok
but suffice to say
our tradition flows deep

THEY LIED TO YOU

they lied to you at the school assembly
they lied when they recited I Have A Dream

they lied to you about "just as long as it is peaceful"
they lied to you with "just as long as you protest like MLK"

they don't want you to protest at all
they want you to shut up

they only made MLK Day
a national holiday to accommodate

they thought "Let's give them 50% off something, & maybe
they won't notice us revoking 100% of their rights"

they don't mind insurrections & rebellions
as long as they are majority white

they look the other way at mass shooters
unless they are trans

they want you to sing the songs
but never believe the words

they want you to buy a gun to protect
your cisgender your Trump flag your family

they don't want you to ask why we had an assault weapons ban
they don't want you to ask why it was repealed

they don't want you to Google how many mass shootings in 2023
they don't want you to count the number of firearms in America

they lied to you about nonviolence
they lied to you about civil rights

they lied to you about Jesus
they lied to you about MLK

that April 4th this year
is more about Trump's arrest than King's murder

that the students & teachers marching in Nashville
will be ignored or punished or both

they don't care that they are lying
they don't care what the books

or podcasts you are studying
say about fascism & nationalism

they said eff your feelings
they banned you from the NFL just for kneeling

they don't want freedom or democracy
if they ever did

they don't care about this poem
because they will never read or hear it

they don't care that you are squirming
in that uncomfortable pew reciting empty creeds

because you know that Palm Sunday
has been sanitized as schoolchildren get crucified

they will be dead & buried in time for
the parched planet that grandchildren inherit

so they sell you the heaven or hell
they promise is better than this land

they are damned just like their vengeful god had it planned
this is absolutely no way to end this poem please grab a hand

we have to fight back to undo every one of these lies
even as another school shooter locks & loads

even as another human another child dies
we have to make this ugly story get untold

do more than protest with poems
may our actions be increasingly bold

[Representatives Gloria Johnson, Justin Pearson, & Justin
Jones are threatened with discipline or expulsion from the
Tennessee House of Representatives for their impromptu
rally in the midst of the morning session on 3-30-2023 as
hundreds protested against gun violence outside the door
three days after a mass shooting at The Covenant School]

MY BAPTISM

my baptism keeps
chasing me around
like a lost & lonely dog

the Holy Spirit speaks
in the gap between
the noise & the silence

I did not mistake my calling so it
sometimes preaches sometimes pukes at
what my heart finds most appalling

discerning my gut & weary eyes
each protester & drug addict & transitioning teen
are the ones that Peter denies

it wasn't about a particular denomination
but those vows of ordination
that I abandoned

have morphed into something deeper that
the body of my religious ache
can never really shake

we think we are the rock
claim to be a patriarch
but only powerful men

are groping
for the illusion
of said power

so this desperate ache in my feet & bones
follows the baptism back
lonely & hungry

ravenous for the justice
waterfall the righteous
love an overflowing stream

I've got these songs on repeat
surging in my head &
some silly Jars Of Clay track

I first heard 18 years ago
gets stuck in that groove where
my grief meets my love in public

resurrection is not apologetics
crucifixion was not a crime
torture is legal &
resurrection is the wildcat strike
the teacher's sick out
the student's walk out

the ludicrous analogy that MTG
made that DJT was Mandela or Christ
was so over the top that we forget

to see a more poignant
holy week analogy
playing out right here in Tennessee

sky Jesus isn't coming to rescue the tyrants
or us but earth Christ the wandering
rebel of love has become

unionized & collectivized
& is ready to break the bonds
of oppression yet again

THE SOUND

can you feel it
I can feel it
can you hear it

I can hear it the sound like the
North Carolina Oklahoma preacher
referenced from an Indiana graveyard

on a Facebook livestream
podcast during the predawn
of a Good Friday morning

about two young activist
legislators from Nashville
& Memphis Tennessee

that sound that sound I can
hear the sound that I remember
even though it is new

it is old
can you feel it can you hear it
it is true

I remember hugging
myself & sitting on
the floor just

listening to the honey
comfort cadence of his
voice his speeches this preaching

was a drug before I realized
the thrill of intoxication
rocking my child self in tears

crying at the tape recorder
crying at the turntable
crying at the television

mesmerized in holy transformation
just a small child crying out loud
at the recording of a minister

why did you have to die oh why
& for years that voice could still
make me cry as I learned to protest

& defy every reason you needed to die
at 39 that was not the right time
13 years from Montgomery to Memphis

but also from Atlanta to Boston
& before that & why aren't we talking about
the influence Howard Thurman had on him

every single day I still shake inside
to think about it so many more articulate
than me have written about him & that sound

of course we are talking about
Martin Luther King Junior who is
only a rhetorical caricature

for the people who have no character
we all know who they are beamed
into your homes by cable news

I wept to not walk on earth at the
same time as King I would later
look to Jesse Jackson or

Desmond Tutu I would listen
& seek that voice that beat my
preacher friend just calls it the sound

the holy sound the knowing sound
don't you know that
in the beginning was the sound

as Toni Morrison would write
to paraphrase the gospel of John
in the beginning was the sound

now 55 years you have been gone
& the world keeps turning round &
we felt it right here in Tennessee

we felt the stirring of the mighty wind
from east to west from hill to hood to holler
the sound reverberating it's shaking souls

I can feel something new yet familiar
in its rumbling down in my toes my
whole being is starting to move

& suddenly the world has caught that wind
at an interval such as Holy Week or Easter
when the veil has become incredibly thin

the power & the sound are bouncing off the
buildings of downtown Nashville from
the pounding rain of Thursday morning

to the sunshine shouts of Monday night
because the Beloved Community is
rebooting once again the revolution is

moving time itself has stopped has shifted
the sky has opened up & the belly of
the earth has spoken too something new

these faithful servants have been studying up
cutting their teeth in the streets from the
autonomous zone of Ida B Wells Plaza

to the grandmothers of Boxtown Memphis
there is a rumble in the land that we
can all feel the Creator's hand on us now

we can say Gloria hallelujah from Knoxville
to the Justins from Nashville & Memphis
they call you the Three you know that you

represent us all embody us all roll with us
to speak the truth to power with us do they
even realize how things will never be the same

with us right here right now you are about
the same age now that Martin was in
Montgomery for just in a matter of days you are

lighting up the national imagination
we are setting aside all past cynical reservation
discarding anxiety for almighty determination

it is coming up like resurrection flowers from
the Tennessee hurt healing generational trauma
fighting back from all the grief & from the dirt

can you feel it that something might be different
this time we are not going to just take it anymore
interconnected & multiracial we are fired up

this time we do not need to fake it we are
the Beloved Community & the spirit of revolution
that presence that sound I felt in that voice as a child

I hear it feel it see it encounter it in your voices
your speeches & sermons to energize & galvanize
this time we organize with everyone for keeps

ABOUT THE AUTHOR

Conceived during the heady year of 1967 in Chicago, Andrew/Sunfrog (he/him) has been spitting & scribbling poetry (under a variety of names!) since the late 1980s, when he was rooted in the urban wilds of Detroit, Michigan.

In the early 1990s, Sunfrog studied poetics with queer Beat legend Allen Ginsberg in Colorado, performed at the Poetry Project in New York City, & offered spoken word before rock bands in California.

After moving to rural Tennessee, in the mid-1990s, the solar toad's poetic craft has practiced its vocation from freestyle ensembles performing in barns & coffeehouses to teaching others in classrooms & workshops, from a campus in Cookeville to the fields of the Bonnaroo festival. After getting sober from alcoholism in 2009, he pursued church preaching & academic theology until the circumstances described in this book brought him back to the marginal fringes of institutions, where he collaborates with friends & fellow-travelers on the edge.

For always, Sunfrog's poems have invoked the Beat-hippy chant & rant tradition, where they exist at the intersections of radical nonviolent activism, spirited disorganized religion, & the chaotic joy of living with neurodivergence & practicing recovery from addiction.

ALSO AVAILABLE FROM
ANDREW/SUNFROG

Previous perfect-bound poetry books by Andrew/Sunfrog include *Beat Is Beatitude* (2014) & *Don't Touch Your Face* (2021). He has also self-produced countless limited-edition DIY 'zines & chapbooks, including the hand-stitched & upcycled recent retrospective of new & selected poems called *Cardboard Amphibian* (2022).

Forthcoming projects include a chapbook of poetry about music & a collection of essays exploring the hippy history of interspiritual theology. For a current list of what is available by mail order only & to inquire about ordering DIY zines or chapbooks, please contact sunfrogandrew@gmail.com.